AKILAH'S JOURNEY

AKILAH'S JOURNEY

Unnah Harper
with writings by Akilah Amapindi

iUniverse, Inc.
New York Lincoln Shanghai

AKILAH'S JOURNEY

iUniverse books may be ordered through booksellers or by contacting:

iUniverse
2021 Pine Lake Road, Suite 100
Lincoln, NE 68512
www.iuniverse.com
1-800-Authors (1-800-288-4677)

Because of the dynamic nature of the Internet, any Web addresses or links contained in this book may have changed since publication and may no longer be valid.

The views expressed in this work are solely those of the author and do not necessarily reflect the views of the publisher, and the publisher hereby disclaims any responsibility for them.

ISBN: 978-0-595-45321-4 (pbk)
ISBN: 978-0-595-89635-6 (ebk)

Printed in the United States of America

*In loving memory of my daughter, Akilah Amapindi.
Though she rests in God's kingdom,
her spirit still lives through me.*

Contents

Acknowledgments

I would like to thank:

The Rainford, Kennedy, Kelly, Dixon and Harper families for their love and strength, and for standing with me through the most difficult time of my life.

Those who have been supportive and helpful in providing information for this book: Stacy Ann Kennedy, Peter Bordonaro, Prep For Prep, St. Andrew's School, Kenyon College, Bob Butler, The National Broadcasting Corporation in Namibia, Leoneda Inge, and Dominique Fontanilla.

The National Association of Black Journalists for establishing a scholarship and trip to Namibia in Akilah's name. And for also preparing to have a monument erected for Akilah.

All of Akilah's friends, her Zeta Alpha Pi Sorority sisters and her boyfriend, Per Orlander, who knew and loved my daughter.

Compassionate Friends of Staten Island for providing a loving space to heal.

All the individuals and organizations for their generous donations.

Lissette Norman for helping me write this book and assisting in the huge task of piecing together all the information needed to build this story.

Last, but not least, my friends and co-workers at Staten Island Care Center, who have been incredibly supportive and understanding.

Prologue

Auntie Jackie got herself ready for the drive into Spanish Town. She wore a conservative suit that she had worn to teach her class at Papine School that day: an emerald green jacket with ivory buttons and a matching skirt. She was tired and she was hungry. The school at which she taught was in an impoverished part of Kingston and most days she used her lunch money to buy food for some of the students who had passed out from hunger in the midday heat. She suspected that their parents didn't give them lunch money because they knew she would take care of them, but she just couldn't sit down and eat her roti and curried goat with all those hungry brown eyes watching her.

So she had stopped home to eat some food before driving to Spanish Town. She lived in Kingston 20, only five minutes away from where she grew up and she made the trip back at least every weekend since moving away.

Now she knew she was going back for the final time. There was nothing left for her to go back to. Papa was gone.

She had to say it over and over again to really believe it. She had been to the funeral, and she had seen his lanky frame look shrunken in the black casket. His face had been distorted. Dwight had told her that his tongue had been distended almost to his chin when he found him. The thought of it made her want to drive her car into one of the shacks along the side of the road so someone would know what was really going on inside her. Inside the beautiful emerald suit.

She drove along Central Road until she could see the road that led down to Central Village. It was so different now. She couldn't see the women who usually sold their ackee and bananas and pears at the corner. The little house that doubled as the store was boarded up, and Jackie knew that Mr. Hall, the old occupant, was long gone. She told herself not to look too hard at the people walking along the streets because she wouldn't recognize any of them. They were strangers. She passed June's old house, but didn't slow down to look in the yard.

When the paved road ended, she continued on the dusty trail that led to the river. As a child, she had spent a lot of time on that river. It was big enough to catch fish in, but there were shallow parts where she could swim safely and splash around with her siblings Dwight, Merle and my mother, Unnah. One night, Merle had come home with a crawfish longer than her forearm and they were so terrified by it, they couldn't eat it and threw it back in the water.

To her left were the remnants of the football field. Dwight used to organize games with the neighborhood's young men here. Most Sundays, people would line up alongside the field and watch the men, dreadlocks trailing behind them like propellers, as they moved the dusty brown ball from one end of the field to the other. Mr. Babu, the ice cream man, would park his motorcycle at one edge of the field and wait for the children to run over with their coins jingling, shouting his name. Now, the field was filled with the rusting chrome of old car parts, plastic bottles and other trash that people had dragged from their homes and left to congeal in the sun.

Papa's house was past Galva's old house and the gully that led down to the still shining Rio Cobre. Along the run-down street, it was the only place that had stayed the way it was. The colorful paint was only slightly chipping and someone had swept up the magnitude of leaves that the mango trees shed. The cherry tree, which perched along the side of the house was bearing fruit, none of which could be eaten because the tree belonged to wasps that had taken up the residence. She could see the separate kitchen in the back, where Mama used to sit pounding the cassava with her mortar and pestle. Sometimes Jackie pounded the cassava and her mother went to the yard to pick scoth bonnet peppers for the evening meal.

Jackie got out of the car and walked inside.

Every move she made sounded loud to her ears, even though she knew no one was listening. When she crossed the threshold, she made a tiny jump over the spot where Papa had died. It didn't seem right to step on it. In a dream a few nights before, she had seen her mother, who had died a few years earlier. Her mother told her she had not been ready to go, it had not been her time. The doctors had failed to diagnose the diabetes that eventually turned her blood to crystal, refusing to flow through her veins.

She stood in the middle of the three-room house and spun around. She didn't know where to begin. She started to clean; sweeping away accumulated dust from the wood floor that Papa had lain down with his bare hands. He had loved this house because he had made it. With help from carpenters and his children, he had built the structure, which so many would call home. It was why he would never leave, no matter how bad it got outside. Within his backyard he would pick a mango from the tree he had grafted from two different species.

"Akilah," he had asked me, "what should we name this one? I cut a Bombay sapling and tied it onto a Black mango one and now they will grow together. What will we call it?"

When she had finished cleaning the living room, she took some of the items that had sentimental value: a favorite plate, the old coffee grinder that Papa had also made, and the cloth napkins that Mama had sewn together. She thought of giving the coffee grinder to me. She always remembered me as a little girl sitting down on the wooden steps that led to the house, turning the metal crank until the brown beans Papa had brought that day from up in the Blue Mountains were a fine powder. Papa would sit beside me with his hot water in a thermos and wait for the beans to be ready. Yes, Akilah should have the grinder.

She walked into his room. It was meticulously clean as usual. There was his bed, a bureau where Mama had kept her things and his wardrobe. No one had ever been allowed in his wardrobe. He kept his belongings carefully stacked in the wooden compartments and at the bottom was the briefcase he always carried with him. She picked up the briefcase, wondering if his intense privacy would stop her even now from examining its contents. She reasoned that she needed to see if there were any unpaid bills or outstanding business. Surely he couldn't fault her for that.

She opened the lock with the key he kept in the bureau drawer and looked inside. It was just as she expected. Papa was a deacon at Bambury Church of God and he kept detailed notes about the sermons and church business. There was a Bible, a hymnbook, pages upon pages of notes about his duties and other important matters. She was about to close the briefcase when she noticed something that didn't seem to fit. It was a stack of colorful paper that she realized were envelopes when she removed them from the compartment where they were carefully tucked. She read the return addresses: "Windhoek, Namibia" and she lowered herself onto the floor in disbelief.

The letters from John, Akilah's father, were unopened and she ripped them open one by one to read them.

Aunt Jackie then shoved the letters into her bag, which had fallen onto the floor beside her. When she got up, she put her bag, that matched her conservative skirt suit, on her shoulder and left.

1

Unnah

◆

"The African Freedom Fighter"

I met John at the Jamaica School of Agriculture through a mutual acquaintance and I immediately liked his quiet and shy demeanor. He had good qualities and seemed to be everything a girl was looking for, but we did not start dating until almost a year after we met. John was a full-time student and I was an evening division student, pursuing studies in English, math and biology. In my early twenties then, I was still living at home with my father.

John was my first boyfriend and the first time he kissed me we were standing across the street from my bus stop. When he saw my bus coming he suddenly kissed me goodbye. I was so nervous, I couldn't say a word and just dashed across the street to catch my bus. My reaction, of course, frightened John terribly. The next day he told me he thought my father had seen us kiss and was worried my father would come after him. We both laughed when I told him it had just been a bad case of nerves.

John had come to Jamaica as a student in 1978 after escaping his village in Namibia. He was among a group of intrepid students, who had been entrusted with the responsibility of forming the Namibian elite after the independence they believed was coming had finally arrived. He had been told that agriculture was one of the fields that would undergo immense change. Once the colonial rule was over, the government would need people who knew how to feed its almost two million inhabitants. Having come from a family of millet farmers in Ondangwa, he felt up to the challenge.

John enjoyed living in Jamaica and told me he wanted to go there ever since he was a child. During the seventies, after Jamaica had fought for and won independence from the British, Jamaican revolutionaries moved to Namibia to help people they viewed as their brothers in their own struggle. From these men, John would learn and immerse himself in Jamaican culture.

I was fascinated by his dedication and found his genuine passion for his country's freedom noble and endearing. Our romance blossomed and in 1981, I learned that I was pregnant. John and I were both happy about the pregnancy. But with John's mission, I wondered about our future. And my fear would become reality when I was seven months pregnant and John received a letter from the *South West African People's Organization* (SWAPO) stating that he had to leave Jamaica to go to Finland. His program had started in Jamaica, where he would study with his peers for three years, then move to Finland for the second leg of his studies. John believed that by the time his studies in Finland were over, the Germans would have acquiesced to the United Nation's demand to free the country and John could move back to Namibia as part of the educated elite. John told me he would return to Jamaica, but he didn't know when.

There weren't many residential phones in the town where I lived so John wrote to let me know he arrived in Finland safely and would continue to write regularly for several years. He even sent pictures of himself and his peers knee deep in snow, a novel experience for him. In one of the letters, John asked me to marry him, but I wrote back with the response, "Not now. Maybe later down the road, after the baby was born and you return to Jamaica." Truthfully, I was not sure if I was prepared to live in Africa so far away from home where John hoped for us to live. John seemed to be fine with my answer and didn't pressure me.

On November 6, 1981, our daughter, Akilah Abaina Amapindi was born at the Nuthall Memorial Hospital in Kingston, Jamaica. Tiny Akilah arrived on a Friday morning. It was quite difficult not having John there to share the moment. John managed to reach me by telephone at the hospital within days of her birth and asked me a thousand questions about Akilah. I could sense his frustration and desire to be with us.

Before the baby was born, John explained that it was tradition for a girl child to be named after her father's eldest sister, which in our case would be "Magano." He also suggested Joan (similar to John) and Joseph if I were to have a boy. I did not like any of the names. I told him I liked the name Akilah, which meant wisdom.

Then in 1983, John heard the news he feared the most. The fighting that had been going on in Namibia since 1968 had escalated and he would need to join the conflict. John left Finland for Namibia, believing he would never make it back.

John wrote a few more times while in Namibia, once to ask me to send Akilah to Namibia to spend time with him. He assured me that his mother would help care for her, but I believed it too much to ask. We stayed in touch for a while after that and then the letters stopped coming.

I never got used to raising Akilah without John, but I made the best of my situation. I remained in my father's house and my father become the father figure in Akilah's life while she became the center of his. For years it was just the three of us living in my father's house. Then when was Akilah was ten years old, Akilah and I moved into our own home. To support us, I worked at a factory, West Indies Synthetics, where I had been employed since I was a teenager. We lived in a new development called "The Scheme" in the middle of Spanish Town, about ten walking minutes from Papa's house.

I was the last of his children to leave the house we grew up in; my siblings had all married and moved away and I envied their freedom. My sisters both continued their education and became respected teachers. My brother became an artist and makes a living decorating storefronts and painting signs for local storeowners. I had been the only left in my father's house and, if I would have let it, that place would have swallowed me whole.

I was born the last of four children to Edgerton and Ada Williams in Spanish Town, Jamaica. Shortly after I was born, my mother fled the family for reasons that still remain unclear and left my father to raise four children. He promptly married Gladys Rainford, who proceeded to informally change the names of all four of us. Though my name is Unnah Elizabeth, I have always been known as Pauline.

Gladys, seemingly resentful because she could not bear children of her own, came down extremely hard when it was time to discipline us. My father, though a less frequent participant in the disciplining of the children, never defended us from his wife.

Akilah and I settled into our new home nicely, but I also had other things in mind. Later that same year, I decided that I would leave Jamaica all together and live in America. It was hard for me to tell my father. I had never been further than a few miles from home before. I believed life was good for me, but not good enough for Kilah. I had heard that in New York, there were a lot of jobs for women like me and I would be able to put her in good schools so I made up my mind to move to America. I had dreams of a better life and also believed I had a better chance of finding Akilah's father once I was there.

My father was enraged when I told him the news. Though he had barely been a father to me, he saw something in Kilah that softened him. I have my suspicions that he was desperate for assurance in his old age, thinking his love for my daughter would buy him the filial devotion that he did not earn. Akilah had also passed a test to attend the best high school in Jamaica and my sister, Jackie, suggested Akilah stay and attend that school. I knew I would have to leave Jamaica without Akilah to find work and a place for us to live, but there was no way I could leave her for long, I wanted her with me in America.

I packed my belongings in two suitcases and boarded a plane to New York. I arrived in the United States in August of 1992 and life in America was different. I had some difficulty adjusting to the weather, to the culture and even to simple things like food preparation. Mostly, I struggled with Akilah's absence. I applied for her passport immediately. It would be eight months before the embassy would grant Akilah a VISA and I could return to Jamaica to get her.

I remember telling her the news. Kilah shouted, "America, here I come!" and jumped up and down. I just shook my head and laughed.

2

Akilah

◆

"Hurricane Gilbert"

We all knew it was coming. People had been talking about hurricane Gilbert for days. We had all been through hurricanes before; seen the devastation and the beauty of the island after the walls of wind and water had washed over us, but this one seemed different. It was September 9th, 1988 and school had only started a few days before. Mrs. March rapped her ruler against the table in front of her three times and we all fell silent. The excitement that had just consumed us dissipated as we sat still in our desks, waiting for her to continue with the morning's lessons.

"OK, who can tell me about Christopher Columbus?"

"He came to Jamaica in 1492 and killed all the Taino Indians who lived here."

"Almost, Donovan. He made them into slaves and most of them died from overwork or disease. How many of you have Taino ancestors?"

A few students raised their hands.

"Well, that is because some of the Tainos escaped slavery and ran to Cockpit Country in the mountains. One day we will take a trip up there to see where they went. OK, take out your textbooks and turn to page 26. Who has read the chapter on the Maroons?"

We hurriedly turned the pages of our textbooks, but our minds were already far away. Outside we could see some of the male teachers bringing large sheets of tarpaulin into the school. They would bolt down anything that could be blown away and cover as much of the school as possible with the waterproof sheets. The trees out in the courtyard were already swaying, even though Gilbert wouldn't hit for another few days. This was to be our last day of school until the hurricane passed.

When school ended, Shakira, Nicole, Dahlia and I walked through the gates and headed towards The Square. We could see Andrea running towards, backpack clutched tightly to her abdomen, the skirt of her blue uniform billowing behind her like a parachute. When she reached us, we could finally make out the words she was screaming.

"There are white people in The Square!"

We all took off, a cloud of blue skirts and flash of white blouses. We ran down the road past the Primary school, past the bus terminal, which doubled as a market, and straight into the narrow path that led into the Spanish Town Square.

"Where are they?" I asked

We spun around and around, but all we could see were the shades of brown we were accustomed to.

"They're gone," Andrea replied.

We must have just missed them. We had heard about these white people, but they were so elusive. Some of us had seen them before, either on television or in the tourist parts of the island, but most of us hadn't. They didn't usually come into the interior of the island where we lived, but occasionally a few would be drawn to the colonial Spanish architecture of The Square. Andrea told us that they would be walking around with cameras taking pictures of the buildings and the people. I looked hard around me, trying to see what they would possibly want to take pictures of, but found nothing.

The wind was starting to pick up and so I said goodbye to my friends and walked towards the Spanish Town bus that would take me home. I shouted, "One stop, Driver," as the bus approached Central Road. The stop was right at the mouth of the road that led down to my house, and at the corner where Mrs. Brown stood with her stack of peppered prawns that I would eat everyday after school.

"Two for a dollar!" she announced.

I searched in my backpack for the shiny coin I had spotted earlier. I handed it to her and took the bag full of shiny red prawns that I knew came from the river that flowed past my backyard.

All around me, preparations were being made for the hurricane. People were boarding up their homes with pieces of wood that suddenly became a valuable commodity. Men walked up and down the street selling these strips of wood, galvanized steel, anything that might stop the wind from blowing away the houses. As I walked down Central Road, I spotted my grandfather coming in the opposite direction.

"Papa! Papa! Where are you going?"

"Down to the Post Office to get the mail. Come with me and we will walk back together."

Papa had been born into the elite upper-class of the island to a family that consisted mainly of politicians and businessmen. None of us would learn this until after Papa died and people we had seen on television came to his funeral. Papa had become a company driver for the Public Works Department and built a modest house for himself and his family in Spanish Town—a place that had no telephone lines and stores were actually the front rooms of people's house. Papa married a woman the color of charcoal—unusual for his family, who tended to marry people with obvious evidence of British ancestry. But for all his rejection of the privilege he was born into, Papa was born for politics. He walked around Spanish Town like a makeshift mayor. He seemed to know everyone in the village and we later found out that, in fact, he knew many of the families on the island. In his days of driving people around the island, he had made friends in every parish.

Every Friday night was Jerk Chicken night in Central Village and Papa was a faithful attendee, with me at his side. Some enterprising men who owned metal barrels had cut them open and fitted them with metal grates to make grills, and would turn the chickens they had killed that day over and over on the metal grates until they were brown. The spicy meat would draw people from all over the parish every Friday. We would sit on the grass in the cool night breeze and break the crispy fried *festival* that came with our meals.

After our meal was over, Papa and I would go down to Mr. Reynolds' store. Mr. Reynolds held popular domino matches on Friday nights and all the old men would turn out for their favorite game. They would sit around the tiny metal table, dominoes held tightly to their chests and take turns pounding them into the table. In the Caribbean, dominoes were not played correctly unless the table was broken at the end of the game, and these men took that rule to heart. I would cling to Papa's chair only long enough to get a sip of his favorite drink, a milkshake made with Guinness, Bailey's Irish Cream, and an indecipherable ingredient called Irish Moss, before running off to play with the other children gathered under the lamps. Papa wasn't an expensive man, but I could tell at those moments that he was at his happiest. It was those same men from the nighttime domino games that he was greeted as he walked down Central Road. I skipped beside him in order to keep up with his long legged gait. He stopped several times to talk to friends who were preparing for the storm.

"You have your steel already, Missa Renny?"

Renny was short for Rainford, his surname. I had never heard anyone call Papa by his first name, Edgerton.

"Yeah, man, I have my steel. I will put it over the windows and cover some corners, but that is it. I'm not doing anything else. It is in God's hands whether we get blown away or not."

"You crazy man? Only the windows? You are up on that hill where the wind is sure to catch you. And you have the river right there ready to sweep you away. Missa Renny, you have some faith."

"I built that house myself you know. If it was meant to stand, it will."

"Alright, my brethren. I'll pray for you in church come Sunday."

"Alright, Missa Mac. See you around."

We turned the corner and walked into the one room structure that served as the Post Office. Inside, a squat sweaty man sat sorting through stacks of envelopes. When he saw Papa, he handed him a stack he had in one corner. As the head of the household, Papa was the one that received all the mail coming into our house and he distributed it accordingly. I didn't know if Mama or any of the other adults had ever attempted to get the mail, but I had a feeling they had never tried. We walked back down Central Road, once again stopping several times to say hello to friends or inquire about the storm.

We walked past the football field where the game had been suspended for the day; all healthy young men were busy securing their houses. There were a few balls from the last game still entangled in the netting of the goal and they rolled around with the heavy winds.

The earth dropped off behind our house, leaving a chasm through which flowed the Rio Cobre. Our house, a small wooden structure, overlooked it. The peach paint was slightly faded by the scorching sun, but there was plenty of shade in the yard under the mango trees scattered along the property. Past the mango trees were the banana trees and apple trees, along with a vegetable garden that my grandmother tended. There were other fruit bearing trees all over the land that we had not planted, but the mango trees were our favorites. Each tree was a different species, some of which had been created by Papa using a method called grafting, which I didn't understand. Whenever we heard the distinctive plop outside our house, we'd all run outside, making a game out of who could find the mango first. We each had hidden the stashes of mangos, adding another level to the competition, that we would parade around to taunt each other.

To the right of the West Indian mango tree was the kitchen, which was separate from the house. There was a stove inside, but there were some dishes that my grandmother simply refused to cook on a modern stove, preferring to make them the way she had been taught. She frequently cooked *bammy* the way it had been passed down from the Arawaks, who had invented the recipe. She pounded the root of the cassava plant until it turned to a fine powder, then after forming it into a dough, she would bake it in wood fire outside the kitchen. There was nothing a stove could do that Mama couldn't do better and she scorned it.

On this day, the hide of freshly killed goat was hanging in the yard. We had not killed one of our animals in a long time, but Papa was uncertain of what would be left after the hurricane. The rest of the goats lay docilely in the shed. They would usually have still been out grazing on the thick bush that grew everywhere humans had not occupied, but the goats had not budged that day.

I walked towards the edge of the land and looked over the precipice. The river was flowing faster than usual, probably from the rain that had started to the north of us, above the mountains. There were usually rafts floating idly by, full of fishermen, but today the light brown water was empty. I would often go down to the river with my cousin to catch crayfish with our little makeshift poles and bucket full of bait. Once, we caught one that was as long as my arm and I begged my cousin to throw it back from fear of being eaten. But for all the sustenance it provided, the river was also dangerous. Shallow in parts, it grew deep and wide as it passed our property and headed towards an uninhabited part of Spanish Town. In the deeper parts, swirling vortexes tended to form and had drowned several villagers.

My cousin, aunt and mother arrived later that evening and we all huddled inside from the now stinging wind. Outside, many of the trees had been stripped nearly bare. The animals were pacing excitedly inside their pen, every once in a while letting out a long bray. They knew the storm was coming and we wondered if they were telling us something the weather forecasters had not been able to predict. But we would spend the next day preparing for the hurricane so we huddled in our little house and went to sleep.

When we woke up the next morning, the sky was almost black with thick cumulus clouds that had gathered over the village. We went to work immediately, putting everything we could inside the house. Papa used pieces of wood and galvanized steel to board up the sides of the house and the windows. He brought his car into the yard and parked it next to the house hoping the water wouldn't rise high enough for it to float away. He boarded up the kitchen, and then the shed, but left a way for the animals to escape in case the water did rise. When he finished, he stood in the middle of the yard, looked around and then walked over to the precipice. There was a thirty-foot drop to the normal level of the river and the last hurricane had swollen it over half that amount. The first few splatters of water had begun to descend and so he hurried his family inside and locked the door.

The rain started coming down hard the next morning. We could hear the steel of our roof reverberate with the force of the downpour and the whole house shook with that vibration. Outside we could hear screaming, probably from neighbors whose reinforcements had already given way. I couldn't hear the animals outside, but I knew they were curled together the same way we were, listening and imagining because we could not see.

Two days passed with steady, unrelenting rain and wind. The sound of rushing water had become gradually closer and more distinct, but the radio announced that we were soon in the eye of the storm. We could do nothing but wait and think about what was going on outside. I tried everything I could to keep my mind off the storm. After I had grown tired of reading the stack of books I kept in my room, Papa came over with a notebook and pencil. He wrote out a sentence in his neat cursive writing and told me to copy it. I sat down and traced my pencil along the paper, trying to make my "y"s with the same curvaceous swirl that he had done so easily. Papa had taught me how to read and write years before my friends had learned it in school and since then taken a marked interest in my development. Sometimes I found the premium he placed on penmanship to be a little silly, but most often, understood the importance of the form and neatness of letters.

When the rains had softened to a drizzle, we opened the door and stepped outside into daylight. At first, I didn't know where I was. Instead of my backyard, there was what looked like a sea of water in front of us. There were fish and crayfish everywhere, which meant the water had been even closer to our house, but had since receded, leaving some of its contents on our doorstep. The river, which now had no boundaries, looked like a highway, which flowed with what seemed like half the contents of the village. There were live animals swimming bravely, but many of them were dead, their bloated bodies floated upended through the currents. There was a man perched in the thick brush that flanked the river with a rope in his hand. When I looked upstream, I saw what he was waiting for; a large brown stallion was heading towards him, its powerful body kicking towards the slower flow near the riverbank.

Even further upstream, a small white house was floating down the river and I could see the occupants still inside. Other neighbors had by now gathered in our backyard, ours having the clearest view of this procession down the Rio Cobre. The men discussed whether it was possible to save the people in the house when they flowed past us, but they knew it was futile. The river had swollen so much that the house, floating in the middle of it, was over a hundred feet away and we had minutes before they would pass. So we watched them float down the river and prayed that they would land safely. The eye of the storm would last for only a few hours and then the other wall of torrential rain hit.

And then one day the rain stopped. The house sounded strangely quiet to all our ears without the pounding. Papa unlocked the door and looked outside before he opened it wide so we could all see what had happened to our yard. The river had advanced upon us only a few more feet and the goats were up to their knees in water. All the inhabitants of Central Village walked up and down Central Road checking on neighbors and helping to clear the roads. Sheets of steel littered the road, along with trees and household possessions. Most houses were severely damaged, but we had been lucky: our house had weathered the storm beautifully. There was a certain jauntiness in Papa's step even as he walked around, lending a hand to the people who had lost their homes.

Almost immediately after the storm, a Jamaican man wrote a song about the tragedy. It brought a smile to the battered faces on the island. The song was about his friend Gilbert who had brought him all kinds of gifts. He was referring to the redistribution of wealth that had taken place after the storm had destroyed many stores and businesses, leaving their goods strewn on the streets of the city. People without homes nor electricity suddenly had televisions.

But the humor masked devastating news. Many people had died in the storm and hundreds of thousands lost homes; mostly the poor whose homes were shoddily constructed. When the roads had been nearly cleared of debris, we drove around the island to visit those who did not live within walking distance. Nothing looked the way it had before. As we drove through some of the shantytowns where people lived in shacks constructed from scrap materials, we saw people walking around aimlessly, stepping over what used to be their meager possessions, but were now scattered and rain soaked scraps in the muddy ground. Several of them came up to the car to beg us for food and we gave them what he had, but it was not enough. One of the men I had seen walking around on the piles of wood fell to his knees and cried.

I spent the next few days wandering around, not knowing what to do. Too small to provide any real assistance, but old enough to read the weary expressions on my neighbor's faces, I spent my time watching the river slowly descend. We had lost a few animals in the storm, whether to the river or to new owners we would never know, but the majority of our possessions were intact. The beautiful mango trees were completely bare, and many looked as if they might die from the torn limbs that were scattered all around. Eventually, we each took hammers and crowbars we had borrowed from the neighbors and tore the wood and steel from the sides of our house.

3

Akilah

✦

"I'll Come Back For You, I Promise"

There was cloth everywhere. I was sitting on the bench in my yard sewing clothes for the doll I had just made. My grandmother had taught me how to cut out a doll from two pieces of cloth then stuff it with pieces of cotton to make her soft and squeezable. Then she showed me how to sew dresses and skirts for my new doll with the scraps she had gathered from our neighbor Galva, who was a seamstress. Soon, Papa would come home and I would help him herd the goats into the yard where they would roam until it was time to go into the shed.

I heard the jingle jangle of the bells first. Nan, the matriarch goat wore a bell because she always led the way, giving us time to open the gate before the rest of the herd caught up. I looked around worriedly for Papa, but he was right in front of the gate, waiting for me to open it.

"I'm right here, Akilah, open the gate."

"Ok, Papa."

I swung open the big metal gate and he picked me up and put me on his shoulder. I was getting too big for him to be able to lift me now and I noticed he kept me up there for shorter and shorter intervals.

"What are you doing right now?"

"I'm sewing some clothes for Natalie."

"Yeah? You want to come with me to pick some bananas?"

"Yes!"

"Alright, let's go."

We walked down to the grove of bananas and looked for the bunches that had turned yellow. I would walk between the trees, looking up through the thick branches and when I spotted one, Papa would lift me onto his shoulders and let me pull the bunch until it broke off into my hands. We walked back to the house

17

with the bunches of fruit and put them in the kitchen. When he had washed the sap from his hands, Papa went inside and started working on his papers for church the following Sunday.

On the way back, I had seen something in a mango tree that I didn't recognize so I went back to investigate. It was a tiny nest that barely covered the palm of my hand and inside it were two tiny blue eggs. I ran inside to get my grandfather.

"Papa, come look at something!"

"What is it?"

"I don't know."

He put his stack of papers back inside his briefcase and lay it on the bed. Running down to the place where I had seen the nest, I screamed behind me for him to hurry. When he arrived, he held the tiny nest in the palm of his giant hand and inspected the tiny blue eggs.

"These are hummingbird eggs. You see how small they are? The mother is probably somewhere around here."

"Hummingbird?"

I couldn't believe my luck. For years I had been trying to catch one of the shiny blue and pink creatures that lived in the bushes behind Mama's pomegranate tree, but they were so fast I couldn't even see its wings. I touched the eggs with the tips of my fingers and felt their smooth, flawless shells. Then Papa rolled them back into their nest and carefully perched them in a nook of the mango tree.

I had just found out that I would be going to America in a few short months and I couldn't be more excited. It was 1993. My mother had left a few months before to get settled and I was to follow. But I tempered my excitement because I knew Papa was not happy about the news. He didn't want to come back from the store and not see me perched in the backyard doing the arithmetic I had been assigned or climbing the tree to pick an especially large mango. He didn't want to herd the goats back into the shed without me and he told me so.

One day, we sat on an exposed tree root outside our gate and waited for the familiar ringing bells. Papa told me why he didn't want me to leave.

"I am afraid, Akilah, that I will never see you again."

"No, Papa, that is not true. I am coming back. I am just going there for school you'll see."

"No, people never come back. They always stay when they leave here. You won't come back."

"I'll come back for you. I promise."

Through my water-blurred eyes I could see there were tears streaming down his cheeks and I used a scrap of cloth that I had in my pocket to wipe them away.

4

Akilah

✦

"I'm here, America!"

The bright images flashed across the screen at a rate almost too fast for me to follow. A little girl was jumping up and down. Swinging around her right ankle was a bright red loop that was attached to a long rod. When she hopped from leg to leg, the rod would swing under her left leg as she landed on her right. It required careful timing and balance, and to top it off, the rod contained a counter that kept track of how many successful revolutions had been made without stopping. According to the announcer, this device was available at the nearest Toys 'R' Us and other fine stores. Its name was Skippit and I wanted one.

As I watched the commercial, I realized that some things were missing from my childhood. By the end of that day, I would count dozens of them. The day before when I was still in Jamaica, the only toys I could imagine were my dolls, hand sewn in brown cloth with cherry-red gabardine lips, my little wooden kart with rope steering that would transport me to all the regions of my back yard, and my little wheel. I found myself wondering, how had I occupied all those hours after school without Skippit? The specter of my tattered brown doll, probably lounging in some corner of my yard back home shamed me.

Just the day before, I had been perfectly happy with little brown Natalie, but that was before the discrete period of my life called B.A. (Before America) ended. What other secrets had been kept from me, I wondered? What world were others living in that I was so closed off to? I felt like a child who inadvertently overheard forbidden, grown-up discussion.

I would spend many hours during the next few weeks taking inventory and things just weren't adding up. On one side was the life I knew, which now seemed to contain a whole lot of nothing, and on the other side was more stuff than I could see even in an entire day of television. It seemed, whenever I woke up, that there would be a new thing, wrapped and shiny, waiting at the store to be claimed. I was measuring and comparing what I thought I knew, to what actually was, according to the glowing box I had come to consider my gateway into this new world.

My first few days in New York were dizzying. The lights outside terrified me. They never seem to go off, even in the middle of the night. It occurred to me that there were people who didn't go to sleep. They drove around outside my window, chasing something I couldn't yet fathom, and they went about their nights as if the sun was shining. I missed the sound of the goats, shifting positions in unison, until they finally, collectively, sighed and went back to sleep.

The next day, it rained, but that didn't stop those strange people from going outside. Everyone knows you stay inside when it rains. My grandmother back in Jamaica hated nothing more than washing muddy clothing. She would sit with her huge basin filled with soapy water and rub and rub until her brown hands seemed to turn gray. It was better to stay inside.

So I watched some television. It seemed infinitely unfair. While other children had been playing Nintendo, I planted peas in my back yard with my grandmother. For some reason, watching those green buds open into tiny white flowers, attached to which were little buttons that would grow into the very thing I had planted a few days before was joyous to me. While others were watching television, I was trying to catch the hummingbird that lived behind our pomegranate tree.

I wondered why I didn't have all the things like the shining children on television with the yellow hair. It wasn't that we couldn't afford them. Every Christmas we would drive into the city and look at all the lights and the store windows full of things in plastic packaging, but we rarely bought any of them. They just didn't look as if they belonged in our world. Our world was one where people grew the food they ate and most of my clothing was made by the talented seamstress who lived on a couple of acres of land next to ours. We ate meat whenever we or a neighbor killed one of our animals and visited our friends instead of calling because there were no telephone lines. In this world, things in plastic packaging seem foreign and cold.

Sometimes we would drive into the interior of the island, where abject poverty has never stopped the kids from having a good time. A favorite game consists of lining up along a designated starting line with a rim from the wheel of a bicycle and a stick. Whoever could push the rim the farthest using only their stick before it stopped or fell over had bragging rights until he or she was beaten. I used to play this game whenever we visited relatives who had no means of coming to visit us. There was nothing like the rush of wind in your face and the sheer force of will that enabled a childishly clumsy hand to keep the stick carefully balanced in the groove of the rim, while controlling its speed lest it go out of control. And when you saw your final opponent fall away, with his rim careening out of control, you showed your mastery by turning around, all the while keeping your rim under control. In that moment, you were triumphant.

The truth was, by the time I saw that commercial, I was the ripe age of 12, too old to really enjoy hopping from foot to foot. I would enter high school soon and needed to find more suitable pastimes. But I never forgot that little jingle, and the ecstasy on the faces of the little children. Would I really have enjoyed Skippit had it been given to me as a child? I'll never know. But I would like to think that the lure of my favorite rusty wheel and the excited screams of my fellow contestants would be too much to resist.

5

Unnah

♦

"Life in America"

Akilah and I lived in a cozy apartment in Queens, New York. Before she came to America, I had spoken to a school administrator about signing her up, and within days of her arrival, she attended Public School 82. She had always excelled in school and I worried that the move would affect her grades. But only months after her entrance, she would come home excited over being selected the Class Valedictorian.

Every so often Kilah would inquire about John. Having told her the same stories of him over and over, I wished to have some new detail to add each time. I know she preferred her dad be with us, but she seemed not to let it bother her. I asked her once, "What happened if your father and I got back together?"

"Do you really think you could get back together?" she responded.

Not knowing where John was or if he was even alive, we could not know the answer to either of those questions. Kilah said she would be OK either way, all she was concerned about was having a relationship with her father.

The year Kilah arrived, I received a letter from Prep For Prep, a preparation program that provides scholarships for students of color to attend a private high school. She would have to pass a test to get into the program and then for her last two years of junior high school, she would have to pass a series of exams to receive the scholarship.

When she interviewed with the program director, Peter Bordonaro, they had a discussion on books so that he could gauge her intellectual commitment, and they chatted about books like *A Wrinkle In Time* and those of R. L. Stine. Then Mr. Bordonaro asked Kilah if she had read any of Stephen King's novels. She was taken aback and asked him in a slight tone of outrage, "Don't you think he's a bit graphic for someone my age?" Despite the fact that he was someone who would be making the final decision on her entrance into the program, she challenged him. Mr. Bordonaro felt she was respectful, but was not going to say things just to ingratiate herself with a person of authority.

The program was very competitive; some parents considered it to be highly stressful for kids, but Akilah hung in there. She would eventually make it into Prep For Prep and earned herself a scholarship. When it was time for high school, we visited and she interviewed with five different schools. Months later, Akilah was selected to attend St. Andrews High School, a private boarding school in Delaware. The school had a population of 200 students and the campus grounds were beautiful with surrounding silver lakes. It wasn't easy for me to let her go away for high school, but I saw it as a good opportunity for her.

In her early teens, I received a call from her friend's mother. She said Kilah had been crying after her daughter's birthday party. Kilah admitted she felt bad that John was not with her after she saw her friend interact with her father at the party. I tried to comfort her when she came home, but the absence of a parent is much to make up for.

In 1994, I met Sean Harper and we began dating. Kilah was a little distant from Sean initially, but it didn't take her long to like him. Sean and Kilah developed a good relationship; they didn't have any problems. She had spent most of her time away at St. Andrews, but in time, she would see him as a father figure.

The day I told her I was going to marry Sean, she asked, "But what about my father?"

It was 1996, Kilah was almost 15, and I imagined that after all the years of not hearing from John she had given up on the idea of John and I being together. I reminded her and she came around quickly. She said she understood and rationed that I was lonely since she was away at school.

"I'm happy for you, Mommy," Kilah said.

Sean and I married in October of 1996.

Kilah came home for summer and holiday breaks. She didn't spend a lot of time on the phone like your typical teenager, instead she preferred being on the computer or out shopping. She wasn't unruly, she was receptive to any advice I gave her, but she hated when I nagged her about cleaning the dishes. She was also very independent. One evening I returned home from work to find her cherishing a pile of clothes she had bought with her very first check, which she earned at her first job. She had spent her entire 500 dollar check on clothes. She greeted me happily and then showed them off to me. She told me of all the sales she caught when she went to Macy's and Century 21.

"I see you shopped until you dropped, huh?" I said and laughed.

"Yes, Mommy, look at all these beautiful clothes."

"Kilah, how about you pick the clothes you really like and take back the ones you're not sure about to get your money?" I suggested. I explained the importance of saving and reminded her of having a means for getting to and from work.

Kilah didn't fight me on it.

"And what if Staten Island was being sold for a dollar, you don't even have that," I joked.

"Oh, Mommy, they would never sell Staten Island for a dollar," she said, nudging my arm lightly.

Kilah was reserved when she left home for high school, but by the time she graduated, she was much more vocal. She was very comfortable with herself and had her own thoughts about how she viewed the world. Being away at boarding school prepared her for going away to college.

When discussing her career path, I suggested she become a doctor, but she expressed that she wanted to travel. "How about journalism?" I asked. In truth, now there are times when I regret having suggested that profession. Perhaps much could have been avoided had her career path taken a different turn.

Akilah graduated high school in 1999 and was accepted to Yale, Columbia and Kenyon College. Kilah chose to attend Kenyon because they offered her the best scholarship. Kenyon was located in a beautiful and quiet town in Ohio.

Kilah seemed to make her way at Kenyon, calling home often to share her experiences with me. She was involved in different school activities and would call home for money. We both laughed when I poked fun of her "money calls."

Kilah was also very ambitious and focused when it came to working and earning money. She would come home for summer breaks with jobs lined up at places like the Federal Reservation Bank of New York, or as an intern with our current mayor, Bloomberg's Media Distribution Group.

Having come from Jamaica, and then going away to boarding school, and away again to college, exposed Kilah to different people and cultures. Essentially, it made her more "worldly." In her last years of college, Kilah developed a love for writing and decided to major in journalism as I had suggested.

Through the years, I could see that Kilah seemed to adjust well to her new life, her new environment, and her new home in America.

6

Unnah

✦

"Over Four Decades of Rhythm"

"Transfa di balance."

"Trans-fa. You understand?"

"No. That not what I want."

"Wait, talk to mi daughta. She can tell you."

I hand over the phone to my daughter and out of her mouth flows the perfect sounds I cannot produce. They seem to flow through the mouthpiece and undulate over the irate banker on the other end, soothing him until he is calm.

"Yes, I will look for those documents in the mail," she tells him. "Thank you. Goodbye."

She hangs up the phone. Within two minutes all business had been transacted and she was back to singing along to her favorite music video. She has no idea how easy it is for her. What it means to be able to switch worlds with the hum of a vocal chord.

I live in a very small part of New York. Small not because of geographical constraints, but cultural ones. It causes people great amounts of stress to decipher my particular lilt of the tongue. I can see their foreheads glisten with the strain of listening to me talk. So I mostly talk to those who are just like me. Luckily, there are many of us. It's funny, but I don't have much trouble understanding the nurse from Nigeria who works on my floor, even though our languages are shaped by hundreds of years of separate people and experiences. Some of her sounds travel through my ears and others go elsewhere, I suspect through a place that knows about our shared experience and historical past. I don't need to strain.

Most of my friends and acquaintances are also from Jamaica, many of whom I knew back home. We form a "city within a city" where we are free to speak in our melody without causing any discomfort. We can gather in Marva's Caribbean restaurant and talk about our people back home and about who will be emigrating. But every once in a while I am forced to leave my comfortable city and join the larger one. I once attended an event for parents at my daughter's high school. It was then I realized that there were other languages beyond the one I had been struggling to master. I could barely follow the conversations of the other parents as they spoke of memberships in societies that I had never heard of. Apparently, American society is just the beginning, there's also the fine arts society, the diplomat society and the CEO society, each with their own language I could not understand. I longed to go back to my city.

I could see it on their faces as soon as that first syllable left my mouth. I reminded them of the ubiquitous nanny that tagged along with the family, still mothering a child who would soon leave for college.

I never copied that staccato authority of their dialect. Nor produced words so tight and defined that no one would dare to ask me to repeat them. And my window has closed. After over four decades of rhythm, my tongue refuses to cooperate.

7

Akilah

◆

"Proof of More Knowledge and Not Less"

"Yes, I would like to transfer the balance from this card to another."

"Oh! No, thank you. That won't be necessary."

"Yes, I will look for those documents in the mail."

"Thank you. Goodbye."

I hang up the phone. My mother looks at me with some bemusement and wonder, and maybe a bit of envy. Many of her phone conversations have ended with me rushing to her rescue, acting as mediator between her and the world. It is a strange role reversal from our usual position of mother and daughter, and usually takes a bit of shuffling for us to get back into position. It's a complicated dance where I make an awkward misstep and she reminds me that I too am a resident of "the city within a city," even though I can travel freely to the other side.

I face the outside world with much more ease than my mother, and I use that to my advantage. I have a retreat from each world in the other. On my first day of high school, I learned many of the lessons that now lie outside her reach. I learned combinations of words and sounds form—a sort of signal, letting the listener know important information. A certain inflection at the end of a certain word can tell you a lot about a person. I was determined to reveal nothing. I would practice certain words in front of the mirror, taking special care to remove the singsong quality of the vowels that characterized my native language. It wasn't long before my words were uniform.

"A wheh it de?"

"Wheh it de?"

"Where it is?"

"Where is it?"

Before long, I had mastered the jaunty, over-enunciated formalities of rich-speak, the dynamic and rushed colloquialisms of my young peers and the modified southern drawl of my African-American friends. I became a master of switching between them, depending on my audience. In my classes, I spoke a sort of English that left no room for doubt about my origins. I knew it was important within my first months in this country. I often wondered about the logic that devalues an English speaker with an accent, even though that accent is proof of more knowledge and not less.

Whenever my mother has to step outside her enclave, I wonder how she will manage. My mother came to a Parent Weekend at my boarding school once and I appreciated it because I knew what that took. The parents of one of my friends decided to take a group of us out to dinner one night and my mother agreed to come. It was the four of us, and our parents; my mother was alone. When we arrived at the restaurant, they decided to seat the parents and children at separate tables, presumably so the parents could discuss "adult matters" and we could carry on with our juvenile ramblings. I could see my mother sitting at the table with people she had only just met, looking very small. She barely spoke, and I knew that she just couldn't see a way to jump into the flow of conversation, the current was moving too fast. She chewed her food and politely nodded and smiled for the entirety of the meal.

Later that night when my mother and I were alone in my room, we finally let out the words we had kept hidden away. Behind closed doors, the sharp words felt funny in my mouth and I let them soften. Little by little they melted and we could finally speak.

8

Unnah

✦

"For What Was Now Lost"

I had been away on a trip and got home late one August evening to find several messages from my sister, Jackie, on my answering machine. The last one urged, "Something bad happened to Papa. Please call me right away." The solemn in her voice dropped through the insides of my chest and pooled in the pit of my stomach. I hesitated to call and instead prayed silently before picking up the phone.

When Jackie answered, she wasted no time to tell me, "Papa is dead. He was strangled to death."

I shot out a bunch of questions, never waiting for answers.

"But why would someone want to kill him?"

"Do they know who it was?"

"Did they catch who killed him?"

"What happened?"

Jackie could only respond with deep sobbing and I cried along with her until she could compose herself enough to explain what had happened.

She had been in school where she worked as a teacher when her husband, Erol, called. He told Jackie something had happened and she needed to come home immediately.

"What is it, Erol?" she insisted.

Jackie fainted in her chair from the news. One of the teachers drove her home and her husband filled her in on the details when she arrived. Three men went into Papa's house the night before, cut the phone cord and robbed him. They weren't sure of the amount, but he had collected his pension money earlier that day and also kept other money in the house. My family believes they took a large sum of money. The next door neighbors heard a struggle, but didn't know what it was and didn't think anything of it. The next morning the neighbors found

Papa's body on the patio floor. Rumor had it that the men had been on a robbing spree and preyed on old people. My brother, Dwight, knew one of the killers and had him arrested.

Before hanging up the phone, Jackie and I wept together, for what was now lost.

Sleep never came that dreaded night. I was up thinking about Papa and how he must have suffered. My heart ached because Papa was gone. And because I was so far away from Jamaica and from him. My eyes burned from the constant tears that streamed from them. All night, Jackie's voice resounded in my head, telling me what had happened and how the neighbors back home in Jamaica talked of Papa's death:

"Yes, one of the men followed him all the way to the store and then followed him home. I didn't know what to think. I saw him walking a couple feet behind Missa Renny the whole time."

"I thought maybe Missa Renny knew him."

"No, he didn't know the man was following him, because he wouldn't have gone home alone. The man had asked him for money and he had given him some. He didn't realize that he was still following him."

"But the man followed him all the way down Central Road. They stopped right there by Fanny's shop. He bought some kind of vegetable, I think. When I woke up the next morning and heard Missa Renny was dead …"

"His son (you know Dwight, right? He lives down there, by that bridge) got up that morning to go check on his father and also saw him on the ground with the telephone cord wrapped around his neck."

"God, and to think we didn't even have telephones until a few years ago, and now that we have them, they killed him with it!"

"Somebody should have said something. This wouldn't have happened. We were just playing dominoes with him the other night and now he's gone."

"How do you know it was the man who followed Missa Renny? It could have been anyone."

"No, it couldn't. Two days after the murder, Dwight was told by a friend that he knew a man who had stolen a stove cylinder and was cleaning it by the river. He believed the cylinder belonged to Papa. They both went down to investigate and Dwight found out that, in fact, it was Papa's cylinder and they suspected he was involved in Papa's murder. Well, Dwight proceeded to beat the man until the police came along and saw them fighting. And it had been the same man seen following Missa Renny the day he was killed."

"Dwight had him arrested, but he's not in jail now, is he? I heard he was living with his sister down in Linstead."

"Yes, I heard that too. The police questioned him, but they say they didn't have any evidence to hold him, Dwight's testimony isn't enough. Some of us need to testify."

"Who wants to do it?"

I felt so deeply for Dwight, who had seen my father's dead body. I understood his frustration at the lack of justice. When he told me about the day he found the man believed to be one of the killers, I asked him, "Weren't you afraid to break your hand?"

"No! I wanted to break his face," Dwight responded, quickly.

Dwight used what Papa had taught him. As a young boy until he was in his late teens, Papa had trained Dwight to box. Initially hesitant, Dwight was an artist and more interested in using his brain. Then when he was older, Dwight saw that he could make money training others to box. He became a trainer and worked with many boxers—some who even came to the United States and are known boxers. Because he had three sisters he would need to defend, Papa believed it was important for Dwight to know how to box.

And Dwight said, "I punched him the way Papa had taught me to punch. If the police didn't come, I would have broken his nose."

The next morning, I was still crying. I had prayed all night for Papa and for justice; that his killers would be captured. And for the gentlest way to tell Akilah. Telling her everything seemed inconceivable. I could not bring myself to call her. *I'd wait until she comes home on her next school break.*

9

Unnah

"The Softening of the Blow"

I would start reciting the speech I prepared to give Akilah about her grandfather alone in the bathroom, and then started over a thousand times. I knew how much Akilah loved Papa and I was desperate for a way to mitigate the blow of his death. Then one night in October, Jackie called me from Jamaica. It had been almost two months since Papa's funeral and she told me that she had found some letters in Papa's house. Jackie spoke rapidly and with incredible urgency.

"And you'll never believe who the letters are from!"

After what had happened to Papa, I didn't think matters could get worse, but braced myself anyway.

"From who?" I hesitated to ask.

"From John! Unnah, John had been writing to Akilah for years and Papa was hiding the letters! There were many letters!"

With the weight of the additional news, I fell back on the sofa where I had been sitting. Jackie waited for me to speak, but managing my next breaths required everything of me and suddenly the living room did not seem big enough for all I had been feeling. It wasn't typical of Papa. He had been such a kind man. I couldn't believe he would do such a thing. Perhaps because Papa had been murdered, I couldn't be angry with him. I searched my mind for reasons why he would withhold the letters and it didn't take me long to find one. I conceded that he just wanted to keep Akilah close to him. Papa feared John would take us away to Africa. Having raised her, Papa felt like *he* was Akilah's father. But Papa never considered the affect it would have on us, especially Akilah.

"I'll mail you all the letters to give to Akilah. There's a telephone number in one of the letters," Jackie said finally.

But I didn't want to wait days for the letters to arrive. I needed to reach John immediately.

"No, give me the address and phone number now so I can call him."

Somehow, the news of John's letters suffused my body with a certain calm. If I were to slip in the news of her father immediately after telling Akilah of Papa's death, it'll soften the blow. *Oh, I pray I can find John and it does.*

The next afternoon, I attempted to call John in Africa and had great difficulty getting through. I was transferred from operator to operator, with the connection often times being lost. I was not going to give up and finally, after almost two hours, there was an answer at the number provided in the letter to Akilah.

Nervously, I said, "Hello, I'm calling for John."

"Yes, this is John," the man replied in a thick accent.

The voice didn't sound familiar so I asked, "Is this John Amapindi, Akilah's father?"

"Oh, no, my name is also John—I am John's cousin," he explained.

When I told him I was his daughter's mother and was trying to reach John, his voice grew with excitement, "Oh, how wonderful to hear from you. John is away on a field trip, but I will deliver the message to him. He will be most happy to know you have called."

I waited impatiently and two days later, John called. I recognized his voice immediately.

"Hi, John ... how are you?" I was happy knowing I had finally gotten through to him.

"How are *you?*" he asked and before I could answer, he added, "How is Magano? I have tried to reach you and Akilah for years."

"I know, John."

I explained that Jackie had found his letters when my father died and admitted that Papa had hidden the letters from us. John initially responded with momentary silence. He said he was sad to hear about Papa's death and went on to ask questions about Akilah. For almost an hour, I tried to cram in as many details of years worth of Akilah's life and John listened intently.

"Tell Akilah to work hard and stay in school," he said. "Education is the key to success."

"Akilah will be home in two weeks. I will have her call you. What is the time difference there?"

"Seven hours," John replied.

We spoke a little longer and John shared that he was married and had a six year-old son named Joseph; his wife was also pregnant with their second child. I told him that I had gotten married as well.

And then John suddenly interjected, "Unnah, I didn't know if I would ever see you and Akilah again. After all these years, I had given up on ever hearing from you."

I didn't blame him and replied, "We'll I'm glad I finally found you. And Akilah will be so thrilled to know where you are."

When I got off the phone, I was notably overwhelmed. I wondered if my body could manage the extreme disturbance it had been experiencing. For days, I didn't sleep, tossing and turning in bed. I barely ate and my husband, Anthony, expressed concern for my health. But finding a way to tell Akilah such knotty and heady news was all that concerned me.

In late October, I had rewritten the speech in my head and summoned up the will to finally call Akilah.

"I have something to tell you, but I want to wait until you get home."

"Tell me know," Akilah said.

"No, it's best I wait until you get here."

Surprisingly, Akilah didn't insist. And five days later, I went to Kennedy Airport to pick her up.

10

Akilah

✦

"Losing Papa"

When the word of my grandfather's death traveled across the Caribbean Sea, up the Atlantic coast and into the cold receiver of my mother's telephone in New York, I was not there to hear it. I was away at Kenyon College in Ohio and I had been calling home for two weeks with no answer. Relishing in my new found freedom, I ignored the sign that something could be wrong.

The year was 1999 and I had only been at college for two months. I was happy not to be in New York, where I had to fend off my mother's effort to teach me how to cook pumpkin soup and curried goat or at boarding school, where I would unsuccessfully try to escape the twice weekly chapel services. I had been at a prestigious private boarding school, which prided itself on its reliance on "tradition"—in other words, heavy regulation. But college was different. There was no mandatory study hall, no demerits for having a messy room—just freedom. For the first time in my life I had stayed out all night partying, aided by the fact that the parties were less than a mile away from my dorm. I would walk back in the early morning with my friends, already longing for the next weekend. The Ohio cornfields had an insulating effect. We had no fear. We rarely locked our doors because we were too busy doing other things. After all, we were at college to experience this unique and celebrated journey: the parties, the all-nighters, the late-night pizza, and the strange conversations with people you hadn't met before. And we were living it.

When I finally got a call from my mother, she told me to buy a plane ticket and come home for my birthday, which was just a week away. After weighing the importance of the parties that I would miss that weekend, I decided to go home.

On November 5th, I got on a plane and landed that night at JFK Airport in New York. A woman was waiting for me by the baggage claim that I did not immediately recognize. My mother was about 30 pounds thinner than I remembered and her shoulders had lowered by at least an inch. She strained to pick up the duffel bag I had packed for the weeklong trip and when I looked into her eyes, I knew.

"Mom, what's wrong?"

"I will tell you when we get home. I have good news and bad," she replied.

But I insisted, "No, tell me now, mom. I want to hear the bad first. Is it Papa?"

My mother started to cry immediately and nodded her head. "He was killed."

My heart sank with the news. We both held each other for a long moment and cried. I wanted to go to Papa. And from where I was standing, I could see the signs pointing to the Air Jamaica terminal where I had arrived six years earlier, alone and clutching my ticket with a brightly painted hummingbird on it. I had not been back to that terminal because the stamp that gave me permission to visit the United States for six months had long since expired and a trip back to Jamaica would have to be permanent. I had been planning to ask him about our family's history.

Papa had lived to become an old man, a respectable accomplishment in most Third World countries, and he was addressed accordingly. Papa was tall, around 6'5" and very thin. His skin was somewhat fair in complexion and he wore brown-rimmed glasses across the splatter of freckles on his nose.

Every Sunday, he strolled in alongside the other deacons at the Bambury Church of God and took his seat behind the pulpit. At the end of the sermon, he and the other deacons would mingle with the congregation, gathering information about who had gotten married, who was sick and who had given up the faith and turned to *obeah*. When he arrived home in the evening, he would sit on the edge of his bed, let his teeth swim in a glass of water on his nightstand, and record the day's events in perfect cursive lettering. No one has ever read these notes because the briefcase was always kept locked, but it gave him great pleasure to create them.

I wanted to know where Papa had learned that a solution of scorpions seeped in rubbing alcohol and bay leaves was an effective antiseptic. How did he know that a black mango seedling, when combined with a Bombay mango seedling, would produce a mango of such superior texture and sweetness that neighbors from all over the village would come to have a taste? Why did he choose this piece of land, so precariously close to the erratic Rio Cobre, to build his house? I wanted to know that he understood why I had to leave, though I had I just begun to understand those reasons myself.

When we loosened our hold of each other slightly, my mother looked at me and said, "You lost your grandfather, be we found you father."

My heart raced and I thought I had not heard her correctly.

"My father?"

"Yes, your father, John."

"Where is he?" I asked, wiping the tears from my face.

"He is in Africa. I spoke to him and he wants you to call him."

11

John

✦

"Letter To My Daughter"

Dear Akilah,

This is your father John Amapindi. How are you doing? I have been writing you letters for many years, but I have not gotten a response. Are you still living in Spanish Town? How is your mother, I hope she is well. I wish I could come and see you, but there are important things I must do for my country right now and I cannot leave. I might not be able to come back. I will tell you all about these things when I see you again. I am sending you some money. I hope it helps to pay for your school. You must go to school now Akilah because without that you cannot do anything.

I have few pictures from when you were younger, but I know you are much older now. Please send me some pictures of you now. Take care of yourself and write to tell me things about you.

Love,
Your father John Amapindi

12

Akilah

♦

"Makeshift Wake"

I didn't know what Papa's funeral had been like. I tried to imagine it, but I could only see Papa standing at the gate, herding the goats inside. Or rubbing my calf with alcohol when the muscle would contract painfully in my sleep, then tucking me in between himself and my grandmother on the nights when I didn't want to return to my own bed. The idea of Papa lying prostate, never to return, refused to cross certain synapses in my brain, and I suspected there were parts that refused to believe it. It was easy not to. No matter the urge, I could not satisfy my need to take the trip home to Jamaica and see for myself. I could not see the empty bed, or the suddenly unkempt yard, nor could I imagine them. Moreover, I was haunted by Papa's killer, a man for whom I had no name or visage, but who made me spring out of bed to test the lock on my door most nights.

My family left the warmth of Jamaica to fly to New York around Christmas time so that we could participate in a makeshift wake. Papa had long been buried, but none of us could rest easy. The cold winter winds were howling outside, yet we couldn't hear them. Inside, we all sat huddled in the living room, shivering not from the temperature, but from the empty space in the room that seemed to overpower even our sizeable number squeezed together. We knew that the only presence that could fill that space would never do so again.

My grandfather's picture lay on the table, staring up at us from his obituary, periodically bringing us back to think about the life he led. But mostly we thought about the life that had been taken. And the fact that no one came forward to testify, there was not enough proof, and Papa's killer was set free.

In the end, we stole moments to share jokes and laugh about things that Papa did. We turned it into a party, played music and opened lots of gifts. We also cel-

40

ebrated my sister, Merle's wedding anniversary. We knew Papa wouldn't want it any other way.

13

John

◆

"Her Third Country Of Stay"

May 2, 1999

Dear Pauline,

I was happy to see the pictures of my daughter Akilah. I was wondering how she grew so fast in a short time. Anyway I was watching a T.V. program here in Namibia about a Jamaican man who did not care about his children. He left the mother alone to care for the children until they are big enough. In my case it is not like that. I love my child my daughter but she is very far from me. If I was near I could care for her but because she is very far even the situation could not allow that therefore I am in a big problem. I want to see my daughter if God allows that.

Pauline I am working but my salary is not so god therefore there is a problem of me coming there because it is so expensive to pay. By air I cannot afford it at all. On your side, if you can afford, the better way is to consult the Embassy in New York. Talk to them give them all my particulars and tell them that our child wants to visit her father in Namibia. The Embassy people will help you with all the necessary information.

Again I want you to send me Akilah's particulars such as a copy of her identification card. I want to make a savings account for her here in Namibia. Since Jamaica is her first country of stay USA is her second and Namibia will be her third country of stay. For that I should prepare something for her as soon as possible. Send it as soon as possible.

Give all my information to the Embassy of Namibia in New York to help find me easily. If you are planning something please inform me in time so that I do some preparations for her.

I am sending one of my photos plus one of Akilah's brother. I will send some again. I want to see my daughter. Akilah is the only daughter I have. No matter, she is very far and what is needed is contact with each other either by phone or by letter. Encourage her to study hard to pass all her examinations. Education is the only way for success therefore she should take it seriously.

With thanks,
from John Amapindi

14

Unnah

◆

"The Certainty of Things"

I could sense the awkwardness in speaking to her father for the first time. It was two o'clock in the afternoon when Kilah called John in Africa. They exchanged greetings and the customary "How are you?" To my surprise, she was shy about asking John anything. She had posed so many questions about him to me and I imagined she would shoot off many of them when she finally got the opportunity.

From her long pauses, I could tell John had plenty to say to her about life in Africa. She loved animals and was excited to learn that he worked in a safari. When she asked about the weather, I could hear her repeat that they have winter weather there too.

Her face lit up when John invited her to visit him. He offered to come to see her if she could not go, but she wanted to meet Joseph and the rest of the family and see the country as well.

"We don't need any shots to go to Windhoek," Akilah said loud enough for me to hear.

And then John put Joseph on the phone to speak to Kilah. In an instant, having a little brother seemed real to her. Joseph told her he learned English from watching television. Kilah was proud that he was only six years old and already knew three languages. Joseph said he was happy he would be seeing her soon. We did not want to inconvenience John and his wife so when I spoke to him I suggest we stay in a hotel. He gave us information for a hotel in his area.

When she hung up the phone, Kilah felt so good to finally be certain of where her father was. She was still grieving her grandfather, but it helped ease her pain. Her smile was almost permanent that day.

"Mommy are you going with me?" Kilah asked.

"Certainly, I'm going with you," I reassured her.

We both had so many questions. And I wanted to see the expression on her face when she laid eyes on her father for the first time; and to know how she would feel meeting him. I definitely wanted to go with her.

Within days, we booked our plane tickets and reserved our hotel room. Kilah was overjoyed knowing we would be going to Africa in two months. When we let our family in Jamaica know we were going to Namibia, they were thrilled that Kilah would get what she had most longed for.

I, too, know what it feels like not knowing what became of one of my parents, and it gives me a great sense of peace that my child will no longer have to wonder about any of hers.

15

John

◆

"All The Beautiful Things"

Dear Akilah,

I do not know if you are still living at this address, but since I have no other I will still write to this one. How are you doing? Did you get the money I sent you? I sent some more in this letter too. Tell your mom to make sure that you buy something nice for yourself. What kinds of things do you like? Do you still love those mangoes? How is your mother?

Make sure you study your lessons. I enclosed my phone number in case you want to call me. I hope one day you can come to Namibia and see all the beautiful things there are to see.

Love,
Your father,
John Amapindi

16

Akilah

◆

"Meeting John"

The airport was small and crowded, with people looking around for their loved ones and occasionally calling out words or names that I could not understand. I looked around too, but I didn't know if I would realize when I had found him. The pictures I had seen of him told me he was a small man. He seemed to be about 5'3 or 4" with no hint of muscle on his skinny frame. And in looking around the room, I noticed that most of the people were diminutive. I wondered if I could even pick him out by his size.

He saw me before I saw him because when my eyes finally located him, he was already staring right at me. I stood motionless about twenty feet away, unable to move closer to him. He was unable to reach me because he was not allowed to enter the restricted area where I had been standing.

"There's John!" my mother finally shouted and grabbed her bags.

I managed to drag my bags over to the short man. He was not alone. With him was another tiny man, also named John, who was missing his left arm below the elbow, and a small girl and boy.

I walked up to John and put my arm around him, not saying a word. He looked older than his picture, but was the size of the average American fifteen year-old. He had gone bald on the crown of his head and around the sides was short black hair with sprinklings of grey. His forehead was wide and his nose distinctive, in fact, very similar to mine. There were lines around his eyes and mouth that crinkled into a smile when he saw me.

"Magano," he said.

That word had sounded familiar. My mother had told me the story of how I was supposed to be named after his sister, as is customary among his people to connect people through the use of names. I could tell by the difficulty with which

Akilah rolled off his tongue that he found it unnatural. Soon, I would learn that the man standing next to him was his cousin and the father of the ten-year-old girl who was staring up at me. I immediately recognized the little boy, Joseph, my younger brother.

We all hugged in the airport and exchanged broken greetings, only half understood on either side, with the rest of the people in the airport oblivious to the magnitude of the moment. Both Johns picked up our luggage and brought it to the jeep that was waiting in the parking lot. We all piled in and made the silent journey from the airport to the hotel where we were staying. I asked the occasional polite question about the language, the wildlife and the people, but mostly I stared out the window into the vast expanses of unlit landscape on either side of the car. My mother and I spent our first night at the hotel while John went back to his wife and two children. By then, his wife had given birth to a little girl, Ndeayapo.

The next morning John arrived early to take us out to breakfast. He had taken two weeks off from work to spend time with us and had borrowed his brother's car to drive us around. He made a very meager salary working in the National Park helping to manage the wildlife, something for which he was overqualified. But he had no choice, as his training in agriculture had proven useless when the changes expected after Namibia achieved independence did not occur. It turned out that the colonialists that managed the agriculture of the country would continue to do so even after the change of rule, leaving my father, with his extensive training in three different countries, to instead scout for sick animals along the dusty roads of the safari park.

John had a smile on his face that immediately put me at ease. His English was limited and I spoke no Ongangwa or German so we made do with stilted conversations about mundane topics, but I stored away every word he said, thirsty for them after twenty-one years. He offered to take us to a restaurant that he said was right down the street and so we headed downstairs and out into the blinding Namibian sun. We had been walking for what seemed like five miles when my mother and I began to get impatient. Accustomed as we had grown to the American conveniences, we had forgotten that other people thought nothing of walking ten miles before breakfast.

John kept insisting, "Right down here. It's very close," as the sweat that poured down our backs and our stomachs reported the abuse. We summoned up our old selves, the ones long hidden that used to walk as if it were only natural and trudged down Independence Avenue to a little German restaurant.

The conversations with my father started out generally, much the way two people talk when meeting for the first time. He would tell me about the wildlife that he cared for in the park and showed me the best places to buy souvenirs in the outdoor market, but I knew there was a lot more to be told. Those stories would come on our journey up north, to his home in Ondangwa, near the Angolan border where his parents were waiting to meet me. He didn't know how old they were exactly and estimated that they were in their early nineties. He made it clear that they wanted to see my face.

"You are my first born and that is important," he told me.

He couldn't quite articulate why and I didn't need an explanation. My father seemed to know almost everyone in Windhoek, stopping to introduce me as his daughter at college in America.

"This is my daughter, Magano."

I smiled and said hello to the faces smiling back at me.

Before long, my father began to tell me stories about how he had ended up in Jamaica and filled in the gaps to some of the stories my mom had shared with me about him. He told me about having to go to war in Namibia with much difficulty and leaving much to my imagination. Perhaps, later, I thought, he would tell me. He described the feeling of bullets whizzing past him as he crouched on the ground, his rifle like an alien instrument in his hands. Death surrounded him. He thought daily of his only child, thousands of miles away whom he could not reach. If he could just find one of those jobs he had been promised, then he would go back.

"But there was no big change after independence like we had expected. Our president was Namibian, but the same people owned all the same things as before. Everyone who was poor is still poor and everyone who was rich is still rich. There was no job for me to do in my field so I got some work where I could find it. I started by cleaning at the resorts, but now I work out in the open land taking care of the animals."

My father had no money to leave his country, no response to the letters he kept writing for years, and no phone to call the little Jamaican village that did not yet have telephone lines.

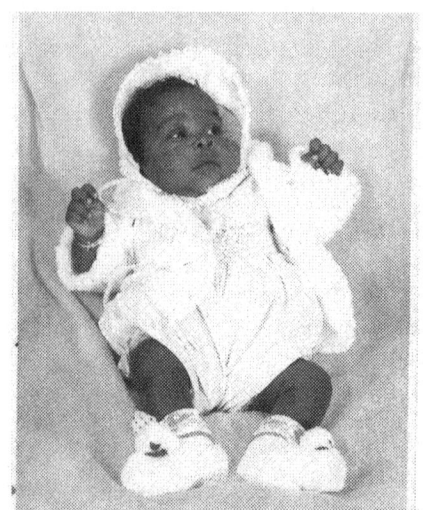
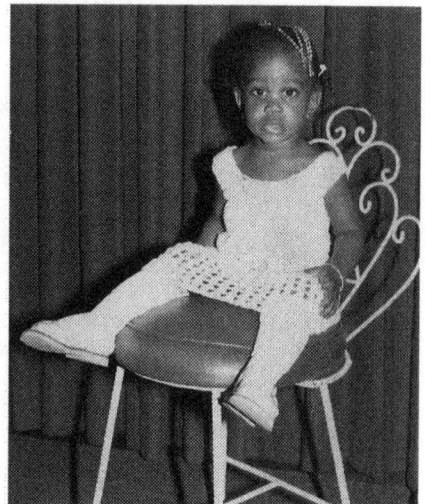

John (middle, right) at SWAPO meeting

Akilah and John

Per and Akilah in Africa

Akilah at The National Broadcasting Corporation in Namibia

Akilah in Africa working on set of movie, *"Nujoma: Where Others Wavered"*

17

Akilah

✦

"Heading To Ondangwa"

Our journey was to take seven hours. We would drive from Windhoek on a road straight to the northern town of Ondangwa, stopping to spend the night at the Okaukuejo resort. We packed the car with food and water for the trip and set out just after dawn that Tuesday. As I sat in the car with my father, I looked out the window at the city of Windhoek with its lone blue skyscraper. My father hated going to Windhoek. Even the name left a bad taste in his mouth. It sounded foreign, even though he was fluent in the language of the Germans, who had so completely colonized his land.

As I looked at the map, I could see that the towns to the north had names like Outjo and Okaukuejo: solid Namibian names. I asked him about it when we stopped for breakfast in a little town called Okahandja. He told me that the people who called themselves Ondangwa, and who also comprised the largest ethnic group in the country, named all the towns in which they lived names that started with the letter O. A sort of signaling system, if you will, that said, "you are welcome here, because we are just like you." In a country where the vast majority of land is owned by colonial foreign powers, this small gesture must provide some comfort to Namibians driving along the lonely, empty roads.

My father would tell me of the days when things were different, but also very much the same. He was a small man and the frame of my own body seemed large next to his. Even though he lived in Ondangwa, he would drive to the capital in the middle of the country to work and to attend meetings with his friends who also had a thirst for answers. They would sit around in an empty room and discuss the events in their daily lives that they saw fitting into a larger pattern. They would read books about Caribbean islands and their economic systems, the ways they tried to develop, and the path to self-sufficiency. At the end of it all, he would make the long drive home, his head filled with ideas and plans, still unsure of what the next day would hold.

Apart from his meetings, he would hate going to the capital. He would have to hold himself as stiff as his tiny frame would allow, lest someone mistook him for one of the blind and downtrodden. He spoke his crispest German to the officials in suits, the bankers and the storeowners, and moved as quickly as he could before the poison of the city could seep its way into his body. He had to tell himself that this was his city and that his great-grandparents could remember a time when it was called Katatura.

He was still telling me about names as we pulled into another small town called Outjo. Here even miles away from where the Germans made their homes, all the signs were in German and Afrikaans, though the people spoke the language of whatever group they belonged to. We pulled up to a convenience store and watched as the local school let out a long stream of children heading home for their midday meal. The mass of brown uniforms and loud laughter retreated down the hill from the center of town. I saw one lone white man waiting in a car and, for a moment, I wondered if he was there to take even more land away from them. But a few seconds later, a Namibian woman emerged from the store with their two children in tow, got in the car and drove away.

When we were back on the road, my father told me about the wonders of the Namibian land. The country is the least densely populated in the world, with large expanses of undeveloped land left for the wildlife to roam. I could imagine him driving along this road after one of his meetings in the city, barely paying attention to the *kudu* and *eland* that would walk along the side of the road. The houses would start falling away in the distance as he got further away from the capital. The white dots were replaced by vast and arid land. To the ignorant eye, it looked like empty unused land, but he knew about the menagerie that existed just a few feet away from his car. They carried out their daily life among the termite mounds and naked trees. Every once in a while a springbok would reveal its striped white and brown sides, breaking the monotony of the landscape. He would drive through the Etosha National Park, which is unenclosed and, therefore, begins wherever the animals choose to roam. My father knew that when he spotted the springbok, the rest of the kingdom would not be far off.

The animals of the Etosha Pan, not unlike humans, formed distinctive groups according to efficiency, my father would later tell me.

"Everyone loves the giraffe. They all want to be his friend."

The elephants, too, enjoyed a special status among the animals and would attract large followings of the less powerful. The zebras and wildebeest would roam together as a group, occasionally joined by some springbok. The other large antelope, especially the ones with large horns, would also roam together, usually a short distance away from the giraffe, who seemed to tolerate his job as an alarm system.

If my father was lucky, he would come upon the large brown pancakes that signaled an elephant was close by. The worse it smelled, the closer he was. The elephant was his favorite animal, I think because he liked the thrill of gunning the engine when it charged. The close escape would provide some relief to the young man, who might not have seen another vehicle in many hours. If he looked out over the horizon he could see the giraffes making use of the sparse foliage on the tops of the trees.

When we arrived at Okaukuejo, we were given a sheet of paper to sign. It stated that upon entering the park, you agree than any personal injury will be solely your responsibility. The park could not pay you if you lost a limb or your life. I could see why this waiver was necessary. The resort consisted of a group of villas, a beautiful restaurant and pool, a grocery store and campsites that were totally unshielded from the surrounding park. We drove to our villa and unpacked our belongings. Later that night, as we stood around the watering hole watching a white rhinoceros taking a drink in the dark water, I struck up a conversation with some of the guides. They told me that a few years before, two hungry lions had left this very same watering hole, walked onto the camp and had eaten two of the guests. None of the guides had been around in the dead of night. I looked behind me at the groups of foreigners sitting around outside their villas, chatting in languages I could not recognize, and thought back to the paper I had signed.

The next morning we got back on the same stretch of road, heading to Ondangwa. On the way, we passed through Namutoni, which was once a German fort. When we went inside, there was a little museum complete with German uniforms, the guns they had used to shoot the Ondangwa people who tried to defend their land, and a small-scale model of the actual fighting. The model depicted a big white fort, the one we were standing in, from which there were Germans with guns shooting at the people on the ground who had arrows. There were hundreds of little brown figures laid out on the turf. I turned and looked out the window onto the manicured lawn and realized that right underneath that green grass, close to the crystal swimming pool and the snack shop, was blood, and some of it mine.

My father too had seen this miniature as a young man, but he already knew what it depicted. His grandparents had already told him the stories. This was part of what drove him to go to the city every week, to sit in that crowded room and talk to his friends. They had so many questions. He was still involved in SWAPO and it was compromised of a group of Namibians who had been watching. They had looked around and seen colonialism take its dying breaths elsewhere, but seem to surge with vitality in their own country. So they secretly organized and discussed the change they knew must be imminent. In the crowds of the meetings would be dreadlocked Rastafarians who would speak of the removal of the British from their own country. It would not be easy, they warned; blood would be shed. My father looked at them in awe.

I have a picture of my father back when he was around my own age. He is wearing a yellow T-shirt with SWAPO across the front in white lettering. His arm is raised and his mouth is distorted with the force of his words. Beside him is his best friend, Martin, holding a banner proclaiming their demands: "Freedom Now!" On a night after that rally, my father was sitting comfortably at home, enclosed in the family compound. Around the group of houses that sheltered the majority of the Amapindi clan, was a wall of tree trunks and branches. The trunks had been pounded into the loamy sand and tied together to form a tight circle around the family inside. It was meant to keep out the lions and jackals that roamed Ondangwa at night and they slept safely inside. This night my father did not sleep peacefully. He had heard that he and other young men in his organization were in danger. Guilty of spreading their dangerous message to the poor and dispossessed in the north of the country, where survival and not equality is the daily concern. "Leave now. They are coming for you. You cannot drive because they will be on the roads."

My father packed as many provisions as he could and left home, not knowing when he would return. He was told that SWAPO had been expelled from Namibia and had to set up temporary headquarters in Zimbabwe and that is where he had to go. He and the others who had been involved in SWAPO left his town and walked south. At night, they lit fires around themselves and took turns sleeping. Sometimes, he would stare at a lion right behind the wall of flames and hope its instinctual fear would quell its hunger. In the morning, they would walk more through the Namib Desert, constantly watching for the glitter of the sun against a tin roof, where they might be able to get some water. They made sure never to enter the capital, instead walking into Botswana, where they were able to hitchhike into Zimbabwe. When they rejoined their comrades in Zimbabwe, they were jubilant. They counted and counted again, to see who had made it out of the country. Many had, but not all.

He was far away from the tree trunk fence, but he was willing to go farther still. A few days later, my father got on an airplane for Jamaica, where he was to study agriculture at the University. The people of SWAPO had their goals in mind. If the people of Namibia were to survive when they reached independence, there had to be people who knew the science of feeding themselves. And so my father left for the promised land.

We finally reached Ondangwa later that afternoon. We drove toward a large homestead with many small houses inside, each with a thick roof made of thatched dried grass. We approached the gate and got out of the car. I walked around outside the compound and surveyed the stretch of land in front of me. Right outside the homestead was a garden, which grew pumpkins, a guava tree, watermelon, beans and corn. In the acres of land that stretched ahead, there were rows upon rows of millet, the staple crop. I would later learn that the family ate the food that it grew and would trade with neighbors for goods that it did not produce.

As I looked out over the land, I tried to imagine my father standing here so many years ago, knowing that he would not live if he stayed. Here, in a place mostly unchanged, there is no refrigerator, no television, no radio; only some people living and eating from the land that they tended. What is it about this that inspired so much hatred in the people who already had everything?

I buried my feet as far as they would go into the loamy soil.

18

Akilah

✦

"My Deepest Connection To Namibia"

It was a deep, reddish-purple with stripes of green and yellow trailing along the torso, hem and sleeves. Made of a fine cotton that was nearly sheer, and sewn with a purple thread, it was barely distinguishable from the cloth of the dress.

Magano had sewn it the week before with the remainder of cloth from her last garment. It was modeled exactly after the one she was wearing, as well as every other woman she knew. It was the traditional dress of the Ondangwa women, and the three stripes running along the delicate cloth was a symbol, to all those who could read it, of the ancestry of the wearer. She didn't know what size to make it. She didn't even know if it would be well received, but she sowed those stripes onto the loosely cut purple dress with faith.

It fit me as if it had been sewn onto my body. As soon as I arrived at the homestead, Magano pulled out the dress for me to try on. She slipped it over my shoulders, over the t-shirt with the elephants and rhinos printed on the front, which I had bought in the tourist gift shop a few days before, and pulled it down over my dusty jeans. Then she took out the necklace made of ostrich shells that she had pounded into circular pieces and dyed pink, and slid it over my head. I was now dressed identically as her and my other aunts, who stood around with gleeful looks on their faces. They were unable to tell me in either their language or mine what they thought of this moment.

The translation, I knew, did not tell the whole story.

"Magano hopes you like the dress," my father explained.

But I could tell by the look in Magano's eyes that there was more to it than that. She took my camera and proceeded to take an entire roll of film of me posing in my dress. One of me standing by the house, one by the guava tree, one with her and Josephina, and on with her and I alone. I posed for over half an hour in various locations, every new position producing a new landscape. My father told me that if I walked toward town wearing the dress, I would be greeted in Ondangwa, the name of the language as well as the people who speak it, and I would be expected to reply in kind.

As I stared at myself in the mirror after the picture taking was over, I noticed my jeans cowardly peeking out from beneath my dress. And as much as I tried to admire the craft of my new garment, the coarse denim prevented the cool cotton from ever touching my skin. In shame, I took off the dress, hoping to gather the courage to put it on by itself. But the courage never came. I feared the exposure I knew I would feel if I removed the pants and t-shirt. Mostly, I feared the expectations on my part when greeted so I folded up the dress and carefully placed it inside my suitcase.

It was then that I realized my three different levels of connection with Namibia, all through cloth. There are my American denim jeans; tough and shield-like, refusing to let the soft fabric of the dress penetrate to my skin. Then there is the tourist t-shirt, which is something a tourist with no connection whatsoever to Namibia would wear. It is a superficial connection, wearing the symbols of Namibia—the rhinos and elephants are a badge of tourism. It also sets up a sharp separation from the people, the dichotomy of me and them, tourist and native.

Lastly, there is the dress, my deepest connection to Namibia. The one that connects me with thread and by blood (sewn by my aunt), and with history (the recognizable pattern). But it was the most difficult for me to wear by itself. I found it difficult to remove my armor—my denim and tourist t-shirt. It was not easy to wear the dress because it would leave me in a vulnerable position and because I don't speak Ondangwa, as would be expected of me. It's not simple stripping off those things you have shielding you to put on something new—no matter how much you want to.

19

Akilah

♦

"The Goat"

Jacobina brought with her a goat. My father had explained the custom of his culture when welcoming family, which surprisingly, is not different from the custom in Jamaica. What was to happen later that day was this goat becoming the welcoming dinner for me and my mother. I was to be sequestered in another room while the animal was killed, then brought out to for me to choose the piece of animal that I preferred. Being an expert goat-eater courtesy of my Jamaican upbringing, I was undaunted by this task. That part was then cooked especially for me and the rest of the family could not to eat until I had eaten and given permission to eat whatever I didn't want.

Later, we drove off to my grandmother's house. I did not know what to expect and imagined it would be very similar to Jacobina's house. We drove for a couple of miles and then once again turned off the road onto a gravel path. We drove for a few more miles and then encountered the same tree fence I had seen before. This time, there was no livestock quarters, but what seemed to be a garden with fruit-laden trees. Next to it was a large homestead, with many small houses inside, each with a thick roof made of thatched dried grass. We approached the gate and got out of the car. Immediately, out came people who I correctly assumed were sibling and cousins of my father. They greeted us warmly in their native tongue, which we still felt the meaning of even though we didn't understand. We were ushered inside and passed through a labyrinth of small houses until we reached an open area. There sat my grandparents. I was told that many people in the area actually lost track of their ages as they grew older, but my grandparents ages were known. They are 89 and 95 years old. They speak no English, but their smiles were unmistakable.

I had been hearing for months how much they wanted to meet me. As the first born child of their eldest son, I occupy a special place in the family. After introductions were made, our bags were taken to the guest quarters where we would be staying; it was the house of one of my father's sisters, who had married and moved to her husband's house. The heat in that part of the country was intense and we could barely find the energy to move around, but my excitement got the better of me. I immediately went out to the garden to see what was growing there. It was familiar to me because in my homeland, my grandmother also grew much of the food we ate. It was economical as well as convenient in the absence of giant supermarkets that sold packaged and processed food.

I recognized pumpkin patches, watermelon, beans, corn, which they call maize, and millet. Millet is mostly used as a rice-like substance. It is also formed into pancakes called porridge, which bears no resemblance to what is commonly known as porridge in America. The grain goes through no processing whatsoever and is eaten in almost natural form. The millet was also used to make alcohol.

There were many other fruits and vegetables, some of which had no English names. Surrounding the homestead for about a mile in each direction was the family's farm. On that land grew extensive crops of millet, with small patches of peas and other plants. This land was unfenced and had no markers. My father told me that it was common knowledge where his land ended and the neighbor's began. There was no need to put up fences around the crop area.

I asked my father once, why my grandparents didn't move to the city where there were the conveniences of modern life. He explained that they had visited Windhoek once and they told him if they didn't go back to the country, they would die. This was the only life they knew and it was the one they chose.

I remember tourists in Jamaica saying, "The Jamaican people are so happy." I wanted to shout out that just beneath the plastered smiles are the effects of crushing poverty. "Happy" is the excuse tourists use to make themselves feel better about the fact that their dollar means the difference between life and death for poor people. So I am wary of people who say that people who live in industrial societies, in poverty, are "happy," but in my grandparent's case, I would have to agree that they are, in fact, happy. And there is a distinction to be made about poverty. My grandparents are not poor, even though they have no electricity. They have everything they need and want. They will never go hungry, they own the land and house that they built themselves. They also have dozens of people who care about their well-being and will stay with them until their dying day. There are many old people in America who do not have these things.

Being there brought on sadness and a longing for my own homeland. It reminded me of how much things had changed. When I was last in Jamaica, I would see people with all kinds of food growing in their backyards and scraping money together to go to the supermarket for something to eat. The people have become so brainwashed, they believe that if it looks like what Americans eat, it must be better.

I picked a guava from my grandparent's tree and ate it, marveling at the fact that this fruit was exactly the way it was intended to be. I recalled that tree days later, when we got word in New York that my grandmother had passed away in her sleep.

20

Akilah

✦

"Going Home"

The last time I saw Papa's house I was eleven years old. I could see a dark shadowy area at the end of Central Road. The gate was still the same, a huge rusting plank stretched across the entranceway, with a bolt to secure it to the tree branch on the opposite side. But there was no sun shining in the yard because of the dense overgrowth of the mango trees. They choked out all the sunlight and left the yard immersed in gloom, even though it was the middle of the day.

"People used to call our house the pretty house on Big Lane. You remember that, Aunt Jackie?"

"Yeah, they would say, 'Missa Renny lives in the pretty house.'"

People would even have their weddings at our house because it was a perfect setting. Mama planted those red flowers all over the place. Hibiscus and some others too. They grew wildly, but just wild enough to be beautiful. The mango trees were always pruned and one of us children would have the job of sweeping up the leaves that fell everyday. There were nine mango trees so that meant a lot of leaves and everyday we would take the rake or the broom and sweep them up before Papa came home from work.

Aunt Jackie, her husband, Erol, and I drove down Big Lane and headed towards Papa's house almost a year after he had died. People along the side of the street stopped to stare at our car and its strangers. Perhaps they wondered if we were the rich relatives of some forsaken resident. I could tell the road had not been paved since I had been away, neither had anything new been built or anything old torn down. The faces of the people outside the tinted glass seemed to permanently set an expression of distrust and fear. Small children rode their bicycles up to the side of the car and pointedly stared at us, our clothing, and the accoutrements in our possession. These were not the children I used to play soccer with, passing the ball back and forth under the streetlight in front of the house until the toads from the river arrived to monopolize the glowing warmth from the lamp.

I remember every Christmas Papa would have a party and invite all his friends from the village. He would have Mama cook curried goat with roti, ackee and salt fish, dukunoo, and escovitch fish. He would pick as many mangoes as he could for the guest to enjoy. He set up tables in the yard, but left enough space for all the children to play. Eventually, someone would bring out an old juice box that had been stuffed with paper and the edges rounded, and we knew the game of Dandy Shandy would begin. One person would stand in the middle of each 'thrower' and try to dodge the ball that was passed back and forth. When nighttime fell, and it got too dark to see the ball, we would light sparklers. The old men went off to play dominoes and the women migrated to different sections of the yard, occasionally fluttering into the kitchen to refill a glass or serve more food.

Uncle Erol saw someone he knew and stopped the car to say hello. It was an old man in a wheelchair who seemed to be waiting for something on the side of the road. He seemed a bit bewildered, as if he didn't know where he was, but he was sitting right outside the clapboard house that was his home. As we neared the end of the road, I saw the little school where I had attended kindergarten. I knew that my teachers had long gone; my mother had received a postcard from my favorite one, Mr. Dietrich, a few years ago that was postmarked in Brooklyn. It was the only place in Central Village that looked exactly the same, with bright paint and cheery alphabet that was wildly out of place in the abandoned Village.

As we neared the adjoining church, we saw two buses parked on the side of the road and a heavy stream of people entering and leaving the small one-room structure. There was a funeral service for someone important enough to have drawn busloads of family and friends from other villages. We didn't stop to find out who it was.

Finally, we reached the end of the road and stopped in front of Papa's house. My uncle motioned for me to open my door, but the tears that welled up inside my lids stopped him. We sat inside the car in silence for a few minutes. I could see the same rusty gate, and a few feet inside the yard, but I couldn't see the house. If I would just lean my head outside the window, I would see the peach colored house that for so many years defined my idea of home. It wouldn't be anymore.

I asked my uncle to turn the car around and leave.

21

Akilah

◆

"They Always Came Home"

Dear Papa,

What is the use of writing this letter when I know your are dead and I will never get an answer? Still, I find the letter must be written, regardless of the outcome.

Do you remember that day when I came running into the yard to ask you a question about the little nest I had found? You came with me out into the woods to look at what had caused me so much excitement. I was so delighted to hear I had encountered the nest of a hummingbird, which had probably gone to get a bite to eat. You took out those two little eggs and held them in the palm of your giant hand. (You always seemed larger than life to me, Papa.) Do you know that I waited all day for that hummingbird to return to her nest? When I finally saw her, it was then that I came to see the world through your eyes. The fact that my grandpa stopped what he was doing to gently explain the wonders of the hummingbird eggs, made more of an impact on me than you will ever know.

When I was in Jamaica recently, I attended the funeral of your best friend at Bambury Church of God, Pastor Kitson. I couldn't bring myself to go and look at his body. At the time, I thought it was because I was afraid to see death. But I now realize that in my mind, I had really been attending your funeral. And seeing him would have ruined that idea.

I sat in the pews and cried non-stop. The other church members looked at me and probably wondered why I was so distraught over a man I barely knew. But I was crying for you, Papa. The fact that no one else knew made no difference to me.

You would be so proud to see what I have accomplished. I really wish you could know that I am about to complete my third year of college. Being the first generation to leave the island was tough, Papa, very tough. And leaving you behind sat heavy on my soul. *The thought that we would see each other again is what kept me going for many years.*

Do you know I feel the pain of your death? Quite often in my dreams. I wake up wondering how my skull was still intact.

I met my father for the first time in March of this year. I dread asking this question because it seems an affront to your memory, but I must: Why did you keep him from me? He is a wonderful man and we get along very well, but he can never take your place. You were the one that showed me the hummingbird, Papa and nothing, not even biology, could change that.

I still have not been back to our house, Papa. The pain of seeing the very place where we share so many loving memories is too much. I do not want to see that door that you opened so innocently that horrible night. I also do not want to see the bureau that I walked pass everyday, never knowing it contained letters from another man, on another continent, who loves me just as much as you do.

Oh my goodness, do you know what I just remembered? Us, sitting outside the gates, listening for the bleating of the goats on their way home. They always found their way home despite the fact that occasionally one of them was made into dinner.

Love always,
Akilah

22

Unnah

♦

"More Time With My Father"

Kilah's sense of wholeness was obvious when we returned from Africa. Her peace almost hummed. I had always known that meeting her father was important to her, but I didn't know the extent of her longing until I stumbled across an unorganized stack of her writings. I would learn of the discussions they had when she spent entire afternoons picking his brain about his homeland and about his culture and customs until the African sun set. Beyond the door, I saw them outside and never realized they had shared so much.

Kilah was most excited when John told her that her tribe's name was "Owamdo." She planned to research and learn as much as she could about that particular tribe. Kilah told me that knowing what her tribe was gave her a greater sense of connection to Africa and her family there.

It was in moments like those when I wondered what our lives would have been like had I not lost touch with John and had Kilah grown up in Africa. She wondered too, but told me years before then that she didn't mind growing up in the United States because she had enjoyed all her school experiences here.

Kilah was sure she wanted to go back to Africa. She immediately planned her trip, especially since her father's cousin was a journalist and told her he would get her an internship with the Namibian Broadcasting Company. She had another year or so to go and couldn't wait to finish at Kenyon. When she finally graduated in 2004 with a degree in Sociology, NBC let her know via email that she could start her internship as a radio anchor in September of that same year.

A bad feeling would not settle in my stomach. I couldn't articulate exactly why at the time, but I tried to convince her not to do the internship in Namibia, to instead work for CNN or MSNBC with whom she had already interviewed. The idea gnawed at my insides, but Kilah had an insistence and a warmth about it. I relented when she said, "It would allow me the chance to spend more time with my father. And it would only be for five months." Wanting her to be happy, I agreed.

Kilah purchased her ticket to Africa long before she graduated. I overheard her on the phone with the Embassy in Washington, D. C. when they told her she didn't need any vaccinations for Windhoek, Namibia. I asked her to be sure when she hung up the phone. Having been to Namibia myself and not having gotten any shots then, I believed it to be true. Kilah crossed it off of her "Things To Do" list. And I, from my mind.

But before going back to Africa, she was off to Chicago to attend Sharai's wedding, her old college roommate. She never could sit still for too long. There was always some new place to visit. Kilah was determined to travel the world.

23

Unnah

◆

"In Exile With Samuel Nujoma"

Before boarding her plane, Kilah called me from the airport and said, "I love you." She had stopped off in London first to visit her friend for two days and then went on to Namibia. She called me again when she arrived on a Monday morning in late September, just like I had asked her to. Her father's cousin, Aune Naanda, would receive Kilah at her home on 9A Lenie Street, Ludwigsdorf, Windhoek, Namibia. Kilah's cousin, Unde, who lived there as well, arranged to pick her up from the airport.

She looked forward to her internship with NBC, which started the following Monday. The Sunday before, she called to let me know how she had settled in her first week and then almost every Sunday from then on. John visited her as often as he could and her speech quickened with excitement when she shared about getting to know him better. She also marveled at life in Namibia and especially loved meeting and speaking with the people there.

Kilah had started covering local stories for both radio and television and also compiled and recorded the economic report for the evening news broadcasts.

With time, she would produce and present the half-hour daily radio actuality show, "Update Namibia", and then moved on to an investigative television reporting program, "Open File." It was during one her 5 o'clock radio network bulletins that Bob Butler, from the National Association of Black Journalists, heard Kilah. On an afternoon in December, he was at the NBC office talking to the general manager, Koamo Tjombe.

"You know, we have an intern from the states," Koamo informed him.

Bob returned to their office to listen in on Kilah's bulletin and was impressed. He thought she had potential and spoke to her about NABJ and their conference in Atlanta, Georgia the following summer. He gave her information to apply for a position in their "Next Generation Radio" project.

When her internship ended in March, Kilah called to tell me she had been offered a position to work on a feature film called, *Nujoma: Where Others Wavered*, about Samuel Nujoma, the first Namibian president and former president of SWAPO. She would only be staying less than a month, she tried to reassure me. I felt she should come home and reminded her that there were other jobs in America, but Kilah maintained that it was a good opportunity and also looked great on her resume. She explained that Sam Nujoma had been in exile with her father, John, and it was basically a story of what they went through in their struggle against the Dutch for independence. They had wanted to make it a huge international Oscar-contending movie and it was really important for her to be a part of that movie.

Then she said, "Mom, I have something to tell you."

"Well, I have something to tell you too," I responded.

"OK, you go first," she said.

"Well, Sean and I are going away to Aruba. Now, what do you have to tell me?"

She said she met a young man named Per Orlander, who was there on an internship as well.

"The only thing, Mommy, is that he's white," Kilah said timidly. "He's from Sweden."

"Kilah, all that matters is that you both care about each other," I replied, chuckling.

Per's mother was visiting Namibia and he was taking them both out to dinner soon. I jokingly asked, "Well, when am I going to meet him?"

"Soon, Mommy," she replied, "and we took some of the most beautiful pictures together. I'll show them to you when I get home."

In that same conversation, I would know just how taken Kilah was by Per when she told me she planned to meet his family in Sweden when she returned to the states. "Of course, it would be after I spend time at home with you," she added.

By then it was obvious that Kilah and Per had fallen in love, basically at first sight. "He's dreamy!" she admitted. "He's tall, with broad shoulders and a swimmer's body because he's been swimming since he was eight. He's turning twenty-three soon. He's still in school because he's in one of those programs where he only has to do one more year to have his Masters in International Development." They had had many of the same ideals and felt the same way about raising children. They had even talked about having jobs where they could travel around as a family and raise their kids all over the world.

However, in an email, Kilah wrote that public displays of affection between her and Per felt weird because that country had been under Apartheid just fifteen years before and when people saw "this tall super-blonde guy kissing this little black girl," they got stares.

Kilah bought her ticket to Sweden while still in Africa. And not wanting to overstay her welcome in Unde's house—she had been living with her for a few months—she arranged to stay with a friend, a woman she met there named Stella. Unde worked for the United Nations and was also traveling out of town so she thought it was more appropriate to stay with Stella.

"Well, what kind of person is Stella, Kilah?" I asked because Kilah was too trusting.

"I think I can trust her. She seems like a nice woman. She doesn't watch television. She has dreads, and she sows and wears long dresses."

Kilah said Stella had a boyfriend who visited her and that John had been to Stella's house and didn't have any concerns. Still, I was a little on edge with her decision to stay.

The movie didn't start in March like it was supposed to because the production company was being audited and they had to account for 30 million dollars that had mysteriously disappeared before they could hire anyone else.

Kilah was excited when the director, Charles Burnette, told her Danny Glover had hopped on board and she couldn't wait for them to start working on the film.

It would be mid-April when Kilah would finally begin retracing the exile of the former president. She assisted a unit manager, who was in charge of organizing all the cars, booking stunts, helicopters, and guns. And the shoot line-up was in Robben Island, South Africa, where Nelson Mandela was imprisoned, in New York, London, and if there was money left, they were also going to Cuba.

Kilah told me she would go in the tent to rest during the shooting of the film and complained about all the mosquitoes coming from under the tent. She also mentioned that Per would go on set to see her and took her out to dinner each night.

She had sent word that Per's friends were visiting from Sweden and he had invited Kilah to go to Cape Town towards the end of April to spend the week with them. She was also ecstatic that her friend, Dominique had asked her to be the maid of honor at her wedding, which would take place in Italy the following year.

She also expressed her excitement over becoming the "Assistant Locations Manager." She worked directly under Mala Vasan, a prominent music video producer, who had produce Jay-Z's videos. Kilah was the person who made the contracts with people for using their location in the film, she decided how much to pay them and secured their payments. Soon after, she proved to be doing better than the "Locations Manager" and took on that role when he was fired.

She said, Carl Lumbly, who played the role of President Nujoma, was a laid back and quiet guy, but lost his cool one day because his mother had just died and he had to fly back for the funeral, he had been in a bad mood.

Then I didn't hear word of her for almost two weeks because the traveling really picked up for the movie and they spent that time filming at the coast. John checked in on Kilah and would eventually call me to let me know she was fine.

Kilah felt she and Per had gotten into a relationship groove that she hadn't gotten into with any other guy before. She couldn't believe how happy she was with him. Per had left Namibia to go diving in Malawi and they had arranged to go to Mozambique when he returned a few weeks later.

She finally called when production of the film ended around the middle of June. A rough draft was expected by December for a special screening. I later learned that Stephen Taylor was contracted to compose the musical score.

My nerves rested momentarily until she said, "Mom, I'd like to stay an extra two weeks to go sightseeing in Mozambique with Per." She spoke to both John and I about going around to see what the country was like.

Jackie called one evening and asked me, "Isn't it time for her to come back into the country?"

"She will be back in a week or so," I replied.

I stood vigil a little longer, waiting for her safe return home.

24

Unnah

◆

"Lost In Africa"

Kilah said Mozambique had no infrastructure whatsoever and because she could barely get any internet access, emailing was difficult. Eventually, she would write to say she and Per were having a great time in Mozambique relaxing on the beach. I would later learn, in more detail about how they had both met.

Per and Kilah first saw each other at a karaoke club, but went out on their first date the night before Namibia's Independence Day, March 22, 2005. Though Per was shy, he was more open then usual to going out with Kilah. They spoke at length and later tried some Salsa dancing, which they both came to the conclusion they were not very good at. After dropping her at her apartment, Per left with the great feeling of anticipation about the future.

They met again the next day, Independence Day, and went to eat at a restaurant called "Something Fishy" where they enjoyed a beautiful seafood platter. Per admitted quickly feeling that Kilah was something serious because they had so many important values and thoughts in common. After the restaurant, they made their way to the bar, "El Cubano," which was totally deserted because of the occasion of the day. There they found a particularly comfortable sofa and spent a few hours talking and enjoying each other's company. That is until all the frustrated looks from the waitress encouraged them to move out of El Cubano.

On one of their dates, they went to the movies at the Maurora Mall. When the movie let out, they decided to go see the monument of the Namibian liberation struggle in the outskirt of town. Weeks prior, Per's car was hit by a drunk driver and the front had been smashed in. As they left the monument, they passed a roadblock—which was routine in Windhoek—and were stopped by the police. The officer explained that his car should not be driven in the condition it was in and that Per needed some sort of registration tag. He followed the officer to his command post to complete some paperwork. Alone in the car, Kilah began to worry about the few guys that were hanging around the road block so she locked all the doors of the car and went to join Per—without bringing the car keys.

The police officer didn't have any tools. Instead, he pointed to the men who began surrounding the car. It was getting darker and darker and Per and Kilah felt at that point that they had no other option. When they tried for an hour to open the door with a steel wire and couldn't, they opted to just break one of the small windows. But that didn't work either. Then one of the guys decided to cut the rubber surrounding the window. That stop cost them three hours, but they got the window fixed at a nearby gas station and finally got back on the road. They laughed it off and headed to the local casino, where they ate and both actually won some money. Kilah, apparently, was falling for him quite rapidly as well.

Around this time, Kilah was ending her internship with NBC and started her new job for *Nujoma: Where Others Wavered*. Kilah had worked hard, and her boss recognized it, giving her more and more responsibility.

Per began to get frustrated because her long work hours interfered with their time together. And it didn't help that he had to leave for trips he had scheduled before meeting Kilah. Per encouraged her to complain about the long hours—she would finish around seven or eight in the evening and had to be in very early in the morning—but she found her work interesting and didn't.

Three weeks before he left for his trip, Akilah invited Per to join her in Swakopmund where they were filming some of the movie. During her time off from work, they took car rides and went to restaurants. And it was upsetting for both of them that soon they would be leaving Africa. They agreed that a long-distance relationship was a crappy idea and came up with a better one—Kilah could go to Sweden to stay with Per. Both of them light up at the thought.

With his internship over, Per stayed in Swakopmund with Akilah for a week and then left for Malawi to travel through most of Namibia and a great deal of Zambia. He would be gone for a month and would then meet up with Akilah in the capital Maputo when she was finished working on the movie. Before leaving, Per and Kilah decided to take the same flight home on the 21st of July when they both finally leave Africa and Per rescheduled his flight.

During his trip, Per began to feel very ill. He panicked when he looked through a guide book and found that he had had symptoms for Malaria. At that point, he thought it would be best to go back home to Sweden, and took a flight to Johannesburg, hoping to catch another flight home there. When he arrived in

Johannesburg, there would be no flights until ten days later. Eventually, he would feel better and continued his travel through South Africa.

Kilah and Per communicated often, sometimes by phone, but mostly via email. She let him know how much she had missed him, and that she was coming down even earlier than planned. Per admitted to being happy to seeing her sooner than he thought. By then he said, he had felt "lost in Africa without Akilah."

They stayed in Maputo for about three days. Kilah found Mozambique to be very much like Jamaica in elementary ways, with sugar cane and coconut vendors along the beach. It was also a big difference than Windhoek in that there was more of a mixture of people there. Black and white people lived in the city centre, making the city feel more alive. They went to a fish market there where you could pick the fresh fish you liked, and then go behind the market to a small restaurant, where it would be cooked for you. They ate everything they could want—lobster, tiger and ordinary prawns, different kinds of fish and crabs. Kilah could not stop talking about all the seafood she ate. She said they had returned to that same restaurant before leaving Mozambique.

After Maputo, they traveled up to Tofo Beach—which took a whole day by bus—and stayed at the Bamboozi Lodge. Their small hut was just behind a huge sand dune that separated the ocean from the land. There was sand and palm trees everywhere and they thought it was as close to paradise as could be.

Kilah and Per spent their days there walking the beach, swimming in the ocean and eating great food at the restaurants sprinkled along the beach. They talked about everything and nothing. Per had written that their love became more cemented in Mozambique and that he was sure he wanted to spend more time with Kilah.

After a week they left Tofo, and a few days later, left Mozambique. They stayed in a Backpacker in Johannesburg for two days until it was time to leave Africa. And while in Johannesburg, Kilah felt ill—vomiting, with a possible fever, but seemed to recover quickly enough to enjoy their last days in Johannesburg before leaving for the airport.

They flew together to London and parted ways in Heathrow Airport. Her plane was leaving just an hour after they had landed. And Per felt that was the moment when they where supposed to say they loved each other. They both knew it, but no one had the guts. If one could only go back, he thought. His plane headed for Stockholm and Kilah's to New York City.

"Isn't that like a movie?" Kilah wrote.

She felt they were getting pretty serious and couldn't believe she had found this great guy at such a young age. She was excited about the idea of moving to Sweden late that Summer until Per finished school in January. Then they would both move to New York together.

25

Unnah

♦

"Cold In July"

I let out a long breath when Kilah finally set foot on American soil. She arrived on the afternoon of July 22nd. I told her to take a cab home and added, "I left your favorite—Sushi—in the fridge for you. I'll be home from work in an hour."

When I came through the door, she ran over and hugged me. I was so happy to see her. Her skin was significantly darkened and I said, "You were really working in the sun, huh?" We both laughed.

"Hey, Happy Belated Birthday," she said.

She had missed my birthday by a week.

"So what did you do while I was away, Mommy?" she asked, unpacking her carry-on bag.

"Well, we went to Aruba just two weeks before you came home. We did a tour of the small island and saw their gold mines." I went on about how all the houses were painted in different colors. And that, at age fifteen, all the children there go to Holland to learn other languages. "They speak up to five languages," I exclaimed. "I was wondering why we saw no children on the road, Kilah, and it's because they're either in bed early or in Holland."

Kilah laughed as I went on about our boat ride and our stumbling upon a Jamaican restaurant there, "Jamaican Me Crazy." I handed her a colorful ceramic picture frame with the name, "Aruba" on it. I thought it appropriate since she loved to take pictures. She, in turn, brought me back African wooden coasters and a bottle of Irish Crème liquor.

"Oh, sounds like you had a good time," she said.

"Yes. Now, sit down, girl. Tell me, how was Africa?"

She moved her things over, sat down next to me and we talked all night. She complained that two weeks before coming home, she had the chills and a bad case of diarrhea, and then she felt fine afterwards.

"Maybe it could be that you were allergic to something," I told her.

Akilah remembered suddenly and said, "Mom, I took some of the most beautiful pictures. I can't wait to show you." Then we talked about her upcoming trip to Sweden. I let her know I wasn't thrilled about her leaving the country again. A few days later, she would twirl around in the living room and smiled. She stopped to tell me, "Mom, I don't think I'm quite ready to work right now, I wanna travel first. She, especially, had Sweden on her mind.

Kilah reconnected with friends and went to dinner with them. The following weekend, Kilah, Sean and I went to Red Lobster—she loved seafood. We stood outside while we waited for our buzzer to go off, alerting us that our table was ready, and Kilah moved away from us, into a sunny area. She said she felt cold, which seemed odd since it was summertime, and July no less, the hottest month of the year. But the African print, backless dress and sandals she brought back from her trip were not warm enough.

After about ten minutes, I called her over to us. It was as if a tiny pebble pelted my heart when I saw the anguish on her face. There was also sorrow in her eyes, I'll never forget. I wanted her close to me and we sat together in silence until our buzzer went off. Before I called her over, she seemed lost in thought and I wonder now if she was worried about how sick she was becoming.

Kilah ordered crab legs, which she usually dipped in butter sauce, but on this day, she barely ate her salad and had only a few spoon fills of Cream of Mushroom soup.

"In Africa you could get a bunch of sea food for five American dollars," she told us. She shared more stories about her trip. And before we could all finish our meal, Kilah felt cold and went out to sit in the car by herself with the heat on.

That Sunday night, we went to the hospital. They had found she had a slight fever and gave her some Tylenol. We left after hours of sitting in the emergency room. Kilah wondered why she had not been feeling well. We arrived home around 1 a.m. and she went on the computer to prepare her work for an interview she had the next day in Atlanta. While she worked, I packed her suitcase. We had gone shopping the day before to buy her some suits for her trip. An hour later, she we went to bed.

In the morning, she had a cup of mint tea and said she'll eat on the plane. I had to go to work so Sean took Kilah to the airport. Before leaving the house, I told her, "Honey, I love you. Just do the best you can." We kissed and hugged each other goodbye. And they left.

26

Unnah

◆

"Isolation"

Kilah arrived in Atlanta on a Sunday afternoon and the convention opened with a reception dinner at the hotel she was staying in. Bob Butler picked her up from the airport and later introduced her to Doug Mitchell, manager for "Next Generation Radio," and her project mentor, Leoneda Inge.

Her first assignment at the National Association of Black Journalist convention was a story on mega churches vs. traditional churches. She had arranged an interview with Dr. Alton Pollard, Director of Programs of Black Church Studies at Emory University, and Leoneda was set to go along with her the next morning.

Towards the end of the reception, Kilah whispered to Bob that she wasn't feeling well and wanted to go to the hospital. Bob, of course, was taken aback and thought it serious if someone as young as her was requesting to be taken to the hospital. Her only concern was that her student health insurance had expired since graduating, and her enrollment onto my insurance had not yet been finalized.

The ambulance arrived at the hotel and carried the weak and trembling Kilah a mile away to the hospital. Once there, she informed the doctors that she had been to Africa, admitted to being bitten by mosquitoes and wondered if she might have had Malaria. She was told the tests results showed no signs of Malaria and she was released from the hospital in the early morning hours, in time for her to make it to the newsroom for the particulars of her assignment.

Leoneda asked her if she was up to doing the interview with Dr. Pollard Monday afternoon and Kilah insisted, saying all she needed was a shower. She didn't feel her best, still they traveled far to get to Dr. Pollards office, catching a train, walking a short distance and then jumping on the school bus at Emory. Leoneda felt Kilah handled herself well during the interview, "Ahead of her years for a young journalist," she told me. Dr. Pollard actually enjoyed speaking with her so much that he drove Kilah and Leoneda back to the hotel. By the time they reached the hotel, Kilah had an incessant cough and said she was tired. Leoneda believed she had the flu and suggested she not work down in the newsroom with the other interns, she should instead go to her room to rest. In bed, Kilah wrote and listened to her interview and Bob stopped by that evening with warm chicken soup for her.

Tuesday morning, Leoneda called Kilah's room to rush her downstairs. They were headed to the King Center to interview the longtime pastor of Ebenezer Baptist Church where Martin Luther King, Jr. preached. And later they would go to T.D. Jake's Mega Festival to hear him speak and takes notes.

"We can cancel if you're still not feeling well," Leoneda told Kilah.

"No, no, no," Kilah urged, "I'm coming down."

After a long wait, Leoneda went up to her room. Kilah was wrapped in a hotel blanket with very little clothing on underneath. She was freezing she said, she had the chills and was too weak to get dressed. Leoneda didn't think twice and called a cab, this time taking her to a different hospital, since there were concerns that the first hospital had released her too soon because Kilah didn't have insurance.

The emergency room was crowded, but with Kilah also having difficulties breathing, they took her into their respiratory unit quickly. Leoneda stayed with her through all the initial testing. As it got later and later, she left to change her clothes, get some food and something Kilah requested from her room. When she returned, Kilah had been moved into isolation and had an oxygen tube placed in her nose. Leoneda put on a hospital gown, a mask over her nose and mouth because they didn't want Kilah exposed to anymore germs, and sat beside her.

"You know I'm not leaving this hospital alive?" she said, with a somber look on her face.

"Oh, Akilah—"

"I know I have Malaria and I'm not leaving this hospital alive. I know how long the incubation period is. And I know how long, if it goes untreated, it takes for Malaria to take hold."

Leoneda tried to calm her down, but there seemed to be no convincing her. She was serious and adamant about what she was saying. Kilah dreaded having passed the incubation period.

Leoneda called me that evening when she returned to her hotel room. She said Kilah appeared to be very sick and they had her in isolation.

"Isolation?"

"Yes, they have her in isolation and they are suspecting pneumonia, but also looking into the possibility of Malaria."

I immediately called the hospital after speaking with Leoneda and Kilah's nurse said, "Their running tests on her and I can't calm her down." I could hear her in the back ground coughing incessantly.

"Let me speak to Akilah," I asked her.

"Akilah, let them do what they have to do and relax."

"They said they think I have pneumonia, Mom—"

With all the coughing, it was hard to make out the rest of what she was saying. I told her to hang up the phone and rest, "I will see you tomorrow. Just relax."

When I hung up with Kilah, I tried to get a ticket for that night, but had no luck. I booked my flight for the next day.

The nurse called me back a little later letting me know she had calmed down and I said, "Please, make sure you tell her she'll see me tomorrow."

All that kept going through my head was "Malaria." It sounded serious and deadly. I didn't know what to make of it. I called my job and arranged for my absence from work.

Wednesday morning, when I called, Leoneda told me Bob and Doug had visited Kilah. Through strained whispers, she spoke to them, she even read the card Bob had brought her.

27

Unnah

♦

"The Lord Doesn't Work That Way"

After dropping my bags off at Carol's house, my stepdaughter, we both met up with Leoneda that afternoon to go to the hospital. The hospital was huge and it took us a long time to find Kilah. They had changed her room to one that could hold a host of beeping machines, particularly a massive respirator.

When I finally saw her, my heart plummeted. The shock seemed to almost paralyze me. Then I began to shiver. She had fallen into a coma suddenly. The loud respirator pushed air into her body dramatically and you could actually see her chest rise and fall. I had not been prepared to see her that way.

"Akilah, can you hear me? I'm here."

"She can hear you," the nurse whispered.

"Kilah, you have to fight. I'm praying for you."

Silently, I prayed the Lord would take me in place of her. I hated the thought of her leaving, but I knew it didn't work that way. As I looked around at all the machines, the doctor came in and called me to another room. The muscles in my stomach tightened. I believed it could not be good if they were asking to have a meeting with me. Carol encouraged me it would be OK. The doctors had informed me that they had a good team of doctors, and explained what they were doing to care for Kilah. And, in truth, I don't know that I was completely present most times I spoke with them. The first doctor said, "Akilah is the sickest patient I have and she's going to be in here for a long time." My mind whirled. I wanted only to pray to God for my daughter and welcomed the hospital chaplain each time he came to pray over Kilah.

Kilah had been assigned a private nurse to stay with her 24 hours a day, and the next day, one of the nurses tried to cheer me up by saying, "I've seen worse cases than Akilah walk out of here and they even returned to the hospital to thank us."

It wasn't until they said she may come around that my spirit settled a bit. I went outside and sat on a bench in front of the hospital. Alone, I began to pray silently for Akilah. Then suddenly, I felt myself slide off the bench and drop my knees onto the hard concrete pavement and prayed earnestly. I asked God not to take the only child I had. But should He decide to take her, I prayed for acceptance because, truthfully, I felt in my gut, that she was going die. I held onto a Corinthians verse in the Bible: "And the Lord said unto me, my grace is sufficient for the weak. For my strength is made perfect in weakness." After long, I sat back on the bench and continued to pray.

I called my sister, Jackie, in Jamaica and she called the rest of the family. I told her I needed them to come to Georgia to be with me and she didn't hesitate.

She would soon walk into her church, interrupt the service and say, "We have to pray for Akilah. They and many of the other churches in Jamaica prayed for her too.

By Thursday they had pumped so much medication into her body that it swelled and distorted Kilah's face. They had also given her a blood transfusion because of all the parasites in her body. I sat in the room while they transfused her. And when I asked about a woman who had moved quickly through Kilah's room with a mask—who did not appear to work in the hospital—the nurse informed me that she was from a local pharmacy and that the pharmacy was also involved with Kilah's care.

Bob came to the hospital and arranged another meeting with her doctors as her health took a turn for the worse. And then her doctor said it—one of the tests showed Falciparum, the worst strain of Malaria. My heart winced. He said her kidneys were beginning to fail and she needed to go on dialysis. Another machine was soon carted into her room.

Still I thought there was a bit of hope. I needed to believe she would get better. I prayed harder. Leoneda brought back blown up pictures of Akilah that she had taken when she first arrived in Atlanta, and we hung them up in her hospital room, "to humanize her," Leoneda said. No one could believe it was Akilah in the pictures.

Leoneda left late that night. I stayed in the hospital and Sean, Carol and I took turns watching Akilah. I tried not to think of my earlier conversation with Kevin, Akilah's cousin. He had gone on about a dream he had with my father, who had gotten into struggle with a woman, but Kevin didn't know the outcome because he had woken up before. And hearing about his dream with my dead father troubled me because growing up, I had always heard that when the dead return in dreams, it's considered a sign that someone would soon die. How rotten the timing of Kevin's dream, I thought.

For the next two days, we stood by Akilah's bedside. The doctor said they would be changing the respirator to allow her to do half of the breathing on her own.

Per happened to call Kilah's cell phone on that Friday and I answered. He said he had not heard from her for a couple of days. It was then that I told him she was sick and in the hospital. He said he wanted to come and be there for the both of us. He was in Sweden and said he could be in Atlanta in two days.

My spirits were low by then. And it would take a phone conversation with my friend Vanya, my co-worker, to remind me of my faith.

"Where is your faith?" she asked me. "You don't have any faith?"

Vanya's mom is a close friend of mine. And her words gave me some strength again.

Jackie, Erol and their children arrived on Saturday. Sean and Carol picked them up from the airport. Jackie had wanted to come to the hospital then, but I suggested she just wait until the next day because the doctor said she was showing better signs in her health.

Leoneda dropped by with food for me to eat, but I had no appetite. I'd barely eaten in days, I slept so little and nervous adrenaline fueled my exhausted body back and forth from the hospital to Carol's house for quick showers and a change of clothes.

"Are you reading the book?" Leoneda asked.

She had given me a book by Iyanla Vanzant called, "Faith in the Valley" the first day I arrived in Atlanta. Though I hadn't read it, I felt like I was "in the valley," which was a metaphor for a difficult and challenging time. I was unable to read much of anything.

Since Kilah was doing better, I felt comfortable enough to leave the hospital and stayed the night in Jackie's hotel room with her. My sleep was light and brief.

And then the phone rang around 3 a.m. I instantly felt weak. I knew something was wrong.

"We need you to come in right away," the doctor urged.

I woke my whole family up.

"Oh, they never called me to come in before, especially not at a time like this," I blurted.

I walked around the room not sure of what I was looking for and then I remembered, "Where's my dress? Where are my shoes?" My knees were buckling up. I managed to put on the wrap dress once I located it. "I know it can't be good." Jackie later admitted she knew in her heart it wasn't good too.

Six doctors were waiting for me when I arrived at the hospital. When I looked pass them towards Akilah's room, her door had been shut. My heart raced. And I knew that instant. The doctors tried to explain that while they were changing her respirator, her heart gave. And the words, "We're very sorry—" stopped all my thoughts. The room seemed to spin and I collapsed onto a chair.

A nurse ran over to me and checked for my blood pressure.

Jackie rushed into her room and kissed her. I could see Akilah from the corner of my eye, but could not bring myself to go over to her. And I never did. I just screamed out from where I was, loud, hoping Kilah could run back toward my cries. I regretted that I had not been there when my child slipped quietly out of this world.

After almost an hour, we left the hospital and went back to the hotel. I left there different, her death had hollowed me out.

28

Unnah

◆

"Somebody in Heaven Loves You"

I sat on Jackie's bed stunned. The past week had seemed like a dreadful flash of time, there were moments where I wondered if it was even real. Prayer could not help me understand that my only child was gone. And most of me went with her.

I didn't think I could pull it together when Bob called me, only hours after she had died, asking me to attend their Gospel Brunch where they would be paying tribute to Akilah. I didn't have an ounce of energy left, but I managed to get dressed and attend with my family.

Days before the brunch, at another convention event, Bob had announced that Kilah had fallen ill. Not long after we arrived, Bob went up on stage, before a huge crowd and sadly informed them that Kilah had passed. You could hear the clatter of forks dropping on plates when he told them. Many were succumb with tears. He shared the story on how he had met her and then the gospel choir broke into song in memory of Akilah.

I cried through the entire brunch. I can only recall saying, "That chapter is closed," and thanked everyone when I went up on stage. Jackie also joined me and shared a few words about Kilah. Then a collection basket that had circulated around the room was handed to me on stage.

Back at Carol's house, the phone would not stop ringing with people calling to extend their sympathy. Leoneda told me they flooded her email and voice mailboxes with messages about Kilah. From there we went to Bob's hotel room to plan the funeral. They asked if I wanted it in Africa, Jamaica or New York and I decided to have the service and burial in Atlanta since all of our family and friends were already there. Delta Airlines kindly donated plane tickets for my family in Jamaica to come to Kilah's funeral.

The day intensified when Bob, Jackie and I went to the airport to pick Per up. Kilah pronounced Per's name like Paar, but it sounded like "Pod" to me. And I can laugh now remembering Bob holding up a sign that read "POD". After a long wait, Per finally called and Bob went to get him on the other side of the airport.

Before returning to where we stood waiting, Bob stopped Per.

"Do you know what's going on?" Bob asked him.

"Yeah, Akilah's sick," he responded.

Bob paused for a second and said, "I'm sorry to tell you that she died this morning." She had passed away during his flight.

Per just deflated with the news. And when he reached us, I could see the sadness on his face, like all their dreams and plans had just shattered at his feet.

Once the initial shock settled, something else happened to me. I went down to the hospital the next day and yelled at the doctor who had treated Kilah.

"How did you know how to treat her?" I demanded. I also needed to know what had occurred when they changed Kilah's respirator. Of course, they didn't give me much information. When I asked why they did not respond to the media's inquiries of Akilah's case, they informed me that they could not answer any questions without me being present or without my authorization.

I called the Center for Disease Control two days after to inquire more about Malaria, a rare disease in America. I became enraged when they didn't appear to know about Kilah's case. I wondered why the hospital might not have contacted CDC, which had been located in the same town, to let them know that they have a patient with Malaria.

The press also called, questioning how the hospital had handled Akilah's illness. Her story was all over the news. And the tears came again when I saw her picture on the television.

The morning of her wake, August 13, we traveled to the Martin Street Church of God for Kilah's home going service. People came from all over and packed the church. Pastor Holston, who officiated the service, mentioned that he had received an abundance of calls with people asking if the funeral for the journalist was being held at his church.

I could see the open light blue casket up front, surrounded by dozens of beautiful flowers. I had them comb her long hair down like she always wore it. I had chosen a pretty, light blue dress days before and never wanted to imagine it on Kilah. I don't know how I endured shopping for clothes she would be laid out in after going shopping together just two weeks prior. People in the store had heard it on the news and hugged me when they learned that I was her mother.

I walked a short distance over to Kilah's casket. I thought, *Oh, my God, this is the last time I am going to see my daughter.* My whole world lay in that coffin and I could barely look at her. I felt numb as I went back to my seat.

Family, friends, and co-workers remarked about their experiences with Kilah, Pastor Holston said the eulogy and a journalist from NBC read a statement John had sent from Namibia. He expressed the grief in losing his daughter just shortly after finally meeting her. John could not make it to America in time for her funeral, but had arranged to come to New York for the memorial service that Prep For Prep had planned.

There was not a dry eye in the church when an audio clip of one of her news bulletins in Africa played and Kilah's voice resounded in the church. Bob had also set up a slide show with different pictures of Akilah in Africa while Per tearfully commented on each picture.

Her good friend, Dominique, also spoke and stated that Kilah hoped their future kids played together. She mentioned that no matter where Kilah traveled to she never lost touch with her and always signed off, "Somebody in Ohio loves you" or "Somebody in Africa loves you." When a black butterfly danced playfully around Dominique just days after her death, she believed it had been Kilah, reminding her, "Somebody in heaven loves you."

Before I left the church, a woman who had heard Kilah's story on the news and felt moved to attend the funeral, approached me. She said she also lost a daughter, who was a journalist, right after graduating from college. She kindly offered to occasionally visit the cemetery and place flowers on Kilah's grave. When I returned to New York, I actually called her to let her know Akilah's birthday would be coming up a month later and she promised to take flowers to the Mount Harmony Memorial Gardens where her grave sits on an open hill.

Reporters rushed us as we walked from the church towards the limousine.

"Jackie, you handle them, I can't do it," I told her.

They bombarded us with questions. "Did you expect Akilah to die?" one shouted.

"No," Jackie responded, "we didn't expect her to die, she was young." She appeased the reporter by answering a few more questions and then we got into the limousine.

I stayed in Atlanta after the funeral to do more paperwork and continued to investigate Kilah's death. While at Carol's house, I told Per, "I think I'm going crazy, I've been going off in the other room talking to Kilah."

But Jackie jumped in and said, "Oh, no, don't do that! Papa used to do the same thing when Mama died."

"No, I don't think it's crazy. I do the same thing too," Per said. He hugged me and we embraced for a long time.

His mom called us from Sweden several times to see how we were both getting by.

When I had done all I could, I prepared to leave. Coming home was the hardest. My whole chest ached as I wheeled Kilah's suitcase, filled with all the nice clothes we had bought together, through the airport. As the plane landed in New York, I sobbed uncontrollably. I knew I'd be starting a new life that would not include Akilah. My heart was so broken.

A woman sitting next to me tried to comfort me when I explained that I had just lost my daughter. After the seatbelt release icon lit up, she passed me a slip of paper with the name, "Compassionate Friends" on it.

"You should join a group for people who have lost children. Every hospital has a grievance group. I, too, lost a newborn," she said softly.

I took the note and stuffed it in my purse.

29

Unnah

✦

"Digging into God's Word"

For days after I arrived home, I thought I had gone crazy. I wandered the streets confused and crying, even pounded a tree angrily. Mostly, I went to the other bedroom in my house alone at night to speak to Kilah. I prayed long hours for understanding, for reasons why my child had been taken from me. But neither were given to me to know. I had always told her, "Put God first." And all I could do was hope she had found the Lord.

Everything reminded me of her. I couldn't go shopping because I thought about the clothes Kilah liked to buy. Even watching the young women shop brought on tears. The grief seem insurmountable.

I called my local hospital to get information about grievance groups in my area and briefly told the woman on the other end what had happened to Kilah.

"Oh, I heard about this case. And when my son was going to Africa, I called the embassy and they told me he didn't need a shot," she said.

After a few minutes, she gave me information for "Compassionate Friends."

I didn't go right away. My husband didn't think it would be good for me. "It would only open up your wounds," he rationed.

When I called my job, they told me to take as much time as I needed, but I needed to do something with myself, to be around people. Staying home seemed worse. I returned to work after five weeks. Ironically, a woman at my job encouraged me to go to Compassionate Friends too. We decided to go together.

The first day, I could not stop crying. The pain was so intense, but talking about Kilah helped me get through it. The group provided a space where I could do that and others would understand.

My longing to have Kilah back encouraged interesting dreams. And where I'm from, dreams come with messages and news, and we take careful notice of them.

I had my first one with Kilah, which seemed too real to actually have been considered one, about a week after I returned to New York. It came on at night while I lay in bed. I couldn't see her exactly, but could feel her giving me lots of kisses on my face, as if to tell me, "Mommy, I'm all right." It was like she wanted to make me feel better. And a month later, she took my hand in another dream and pulled me into the house. We both laid on the bed, on our backs, and talked for what seemed like an hour. She asked me, "Do you remember when I caught the disease? I had to see a lot of doctors, this doctor and that doctor …" as if I had not been in the hospital with her. I still had not gotten an official report about her death, but in the dream, I seemed to get the autopsy results directly from Kilah.

I couldn't grasp the idea that I would never see Kilah again. I kept wanting her to call, to come home again. She had been away at school for the past eight years, I kept wanting to believe she was still away at school. I was in complete denial. Perhaps the desire was so strong that it brought on a dream where she would tell me, "But mom I died, I died."

And then a more interesting dream came when I had only had thoughts of writing a book about Kilah's life. I briefly mentioned the idea to a friend. Then one night, I dreamt that Kilah came over to me, apparently happy and said, "Listen to this, Mom." She handed me a cell phone and also put her face near the phone so we can both listen to a message play back. It was the voice of the friend I had spoken to about writing this book, but in the dream Kilah said, "It's the editor." I woke up believing she knew I planned to write this book. She had also rubbed her face against mine in a playful manner and I told her, "Kilah, you know that I love. Please don't do this to me."

And it was no coincidence that, while sorting through her belongings months after she died, I found the stack of her writings. They were essays she had written in college. Most of the typed pages were lose and out of order, except for some she had grouped together, as if preparing a manuscript about her life experiences. I had considered telling Akilah's story for many reasons, but it was her collection of essays that urged me to finish what she started. I remembered, a few years ago, when she told me she would one day write a book. I had asked her what she was going to write her book about and she said, "You, mommy." I now find it ironic that it is me who is writing a book about my precious child.

People kept calling me to give their sympathies for months after Kilah died. It was good to hear them tell me stories about their experiences with her, but it also brought me sorrow. It was so difficult to have to repeat what had happened to her each time, but I did so because I knew people were concerned. I also received cards and checks. One card actually came from the Embassy of Namibia in Washington D. C., but I didn't respond. I still wondered why they had told my daughter she did not need a shot for Malaria.

Two months later, Kilah's college friends, Julie and Elizabeth, called from Boston to let me know they were coming to visit me. They got lost on the way and almost didn't make it, but I encouraged them to still come. It had gotten so late by the time they arrived and they informed me they would be staying in a motel, but I insisted they spend the night at our house. We stayed up all night sharing stories and joking about how Kilah was, and I felt a sense of peace, as if Kilah had been there with us. Before going to bed, Elizabeth sat down on my bed and said, "You know, Akilah told me once, 'I don't know what I would do if I ever lost my mother.'" She had also been troubled by Kilah's early release from the first hospital she went to in Atlanta and said, "I was in the hospital the other day. I had a high fever and they kept me in the hospital." It didn't make sense to either of us.

The next day, they took Sean and I out to lunch. When we returned to the house, Elizabeth and Julie went to the car and then came into the house, with Julie hiding something behind her back. It wasn't until they were ready to leave that they handed me a framed poem written by Elizabeth, with a drawing of Kilah, and a check, which I did not want to accept. I was so moved by the poem and drawing. We spent that evening talking more about Kilah, and even broke down crying a few times. It was comforting to have someone else who loved my daughter share memories of her. Their visit had cheered me up.

Per also called from Sweden to see how I was doing. After he left Africa, he had gone back to Sweden to attend school. He told me he had been looking forward to visiting Jamaica with Akilah and her visiting Sweden. One day, I asked him what had he learned from Kilah.

"How to eat slower, he said, chuckling, "because I eat real fast."

We both laughed.

"Kilah said I ate fast too," I told him.

They seemed to be such a lovely couple and he expressed that Kilah will always live on in his heart. It pleases my heart knowing that Kilah loved and was loved before she passed.

New Year's was tough. I wasn't looking forward to the New Year's celebration. It had always been a big thing for Kilah, seeing the ball drop and also meeting up with her friend. Every year at that time, I'd listen for her in the middle of the night, coming home after hanging out, having dinner and partying to bringing in the new year. The first New Year's without her, I imagined her still coming home late after a great evening with her friends. But her car never pulled up, her key never turned the lock and New Year's wasn't what it used to be.

I thought it would be helpful to go back home. When the plane landed in Jamaica, I thought of Kilah and tried to hold myself together. It was April 2006, and as I got my first whiff of the Caribbean-scented air, all of the sadness came suddenly. It seemed odd visiting without her.

As I walked through our town, I saw Kilah as a young girl again in my mind, running down streets she used to run down, playing in the yard, and by the church. Jamaica could not be the same without Kilah. And also without Papa.

By the time I reached Jamaica, I was emotionally spent. I wanted to relax and not have to think much about anything. But when I arrived, my brother, Dwight, shared some unexpected news. It amazed me that I would take this trip, during the time I was writing this book, and would get the news that, just days before I arrived, one of my father's killers was arrested and sentenced to life in prison. It was the same man Dwight had caught and turned in, but was released because lack of evidence. He was a notorious serial killer, who had terrorized our town for years. One of the other men that killed Papa was killed by the police during a robbery attempt. And the third killer was never captured.

It was the best news I had heard in a long time. I felt like God had answered my prayers for justice for my father. I believe the purpose of my trip was to finally get closure with my father's death.

I had only to deal with closure for Kilah's. But I suspected it would be a long time before that day came. I did my share of questioning her loss. Why some one so young, with so much promise could die? I thought I could find the answers for why by digging into God's word. I continued to pray and read the different scriptures of the Bible. When she was born and the nurse handed her over to me, I knew I had to raise her alone. I had never done anything like it before and so I called on God to help me. I hadn't even inspected her by counting to make sure she had ten fingers and ten toes before I began praying. I asked the Lord that he guide me in raising her the way He wanted me to, that He be in control of her life, that she go through the world in a good and gentle way. My friend at work said that might have been why God took her the way He did, that I had handed her over to Him a long time ago and He took her when He saw fit.

I've grown tired of wondering why. I lost plenty of sleep and a significant amount of weight as well. And all I know for sure is that sometimes you just have to let it go, death is a natural thing.

I find my peace knowing I gave Kilah lots of love; she knew I loved her.

I've found some while writing this book. I've also been experiencing small amounts of peace with time. I find it in the way others keep her memory alive. I was honored to attend the Journalists Memorial Rededication ceremony on May 3, 2006 in Washington, D. C. Kilah's name was added to the memorial for journalists who gave their lives reporting the news. I brushed her name, which had been etched into the glass memorial wall with the tips of my fingers and cried intensely. She was the youngest journalist added to the memorial that year.

And it brought me peace that her life had not been ignored. In 2006, NABJ also did a trip to Namibia in her name. Kenyon College held a memorial service for Kilah. Prep for Prep also held a memorial for her in New York City when I returned from Atlanta, and they received a generous gift in memory of her.

John came to America to attend the Prep for Prep memorial service. Sadly, a month after John returned to Africa, his wife's baby had died at birth. In a matter of just months, he had lost two daughters and John was so distraught by both deaths.

I find comfort when recalling the little things about her; finding her often under the mango tree reading when she was a little girl; how she sucked her lip and Papa would say, "Let go that lip." And how she always finished her homework before coming home from school; how she busied herself making baskets and forming dolls out of mud; when she learned sign language from my sister, Merle; and how much she loved to play scrabble. I think of our conversations, when she promised to take me to Spain. I told her I didn't speak Spanish, but she said she could help me since she was fluent in Spanish.

I also find comfort remembering the sound of her laughter, and in a tiny passage titled, "We Will See Our Loved Ones Again," that one of Kilah's friends gave me. And in my decision to move down to Atlanta with my husband. I knew well where her journey had started, and I needed to be closer to Kilah's resting place, where her journey had ended too soon.

Akilah,
You loved the frosting from the tops of cakes
so much that you would grab two or three from
the Gund cafeteria cake stands. With a surgeon's
prowess you would neatly skim off the entire top layer
of confectionary goodness of each cake, constructing
a giant pile of frosting which you would consume
one full finger at a time.

Your cheeks would swell and arc with laughter following
a well planned punch line.

You would turn the heat up to a tropical 85 degrees
and hop in bed, swaddled little a new-born under
layers of flannel covers.

You could consume 5,000 calories (of burgers, fried
mushrooms and chicken fingers) and still maintain your
breathtaking sinewy form.

Returning from the laborious late night lectures
(you know the ones!) your laughter would penetrate
the ramshackle walls of our dilapidated Belexy "palace"
and make its way down middle path to welcome me
home.

You loved your favorite songs and too shy to sing
in any chore, you would belt out the notes from
the confines of your bedroom. And I an eager
audience would promptly turn off my music and
stand quietly to hear the rich hued and gloriously
lyrical Amapindi version of a Bob Marley classic.

You see, I am still talking to you as if you were still here, as if your life hadn't been taken so suddenly and tragically, as if any minute now you could bound across the hall and burst into my room to offer me a juicy morsel of gossip which you collected during your day.

I can't hold you or tell you goodbye or the that one last laugh, all I can do is place your memory carefully into a place in my heart where it will remain untouched and untarnished by time.

Love, Elizabeth

978-0-595-45321-4
0-595-45321-X